THE ARMY

CA...CE

idea

Library Learning Information

Idea Store®
Whitechapel
321 Whitechapel Road
London E1 1BU

020 7364 4332
www.ideastore.co.uk

Created and managed by
Tower Hamlets Council

On 5 and 6 June 2009, hundreds of army cadets took part in the 65th D-Day Anniversary. The cadets performed many roles during this event, including marching with the veterans, lining the routes for the VIPs, escorting those who were frail, assisting the French Gendarmes in providing crowd control and most importantly, attending commemoration ceremonies at Colville Montgomery, Bayeux Commonwealth Cemetery, and Arromanches. Here Cadets from 201 Harrow enjoy the company of D-Day veterans on a Normandy beach.

THE 150TH ANNIVERSARY CELEBRATION

THE ARMY CADET FORCE

A PICTORIAL HISTORY OF THE ACF AND CCF

MIKE RYAN

The
History
Press

Learning more about the ACF

The ACF has its own magazine, – *Army Cadet*. There are numerous County web sites as well as the official, central one – armycadets.com. The MoD publishes a magazine called *Camouflage*, aimed at teenagers interested in both the ACF and the Army.

This book is dedicated to the memory of the following Officers, NCOs, Cadets and Patrons from Middx & NW London ACF I have personally known during my service and who have now sadly passed away: Colonel Tony Salter, Major Ray Jones, Lt Barry Robinson, SSI Justin Thatcher, SI Lee Coade, Cadets Dean Preston, Aaron Pond, Charlotte Taylor and Cadet Patron Richard Melville-Coe.

Gone but not forgotten.

First published 2009

The History Press
The Mill, Brimscombe Port
Stroud, Gloucestershire, GL5 2QG
www.thehistorypress.co.uk

© Mike Ryan, 2009

The right of Mike Ryan to be identified as the Author
of this work has been asserted in accordance with the
Copyrights, Designs and Patents Act 1988.

British Library Cataloguing in Publication Data.
A catalogue record for this book is available from the British Library.

ISBN 978 0 7524 5067 4

Typesetting and origination by The History Press
Printed in Great Britain

CONTENTS

ACKNOWLEDGEMENTS

The following people, ACF Counties, Detachments, Companies, Schools and Organisations have my grateful thanks.

Cadets Babri, Costello, Katta, McCreesh and Ryan; Sgt Maj Clahar 202 RE Acton, Peter Robinson MA, Derbyshire ACF, Middx & NW ACF, Powys ACF, Surrey ACF, 201 RAMC (Harrow), Harrow Rifle Corps, Harrow School, Hurstpierpoint College, Victoria College, AAC, ACFA, BBC ,HKAC, RCAC, Avpro and the Ministry of Defence.

Sincere thanks to Canon Alan Hughes, Richard Dickson, Charlotte Hopkins, Sheridan Bratt, Ken Molyneux-Carter, W02 Chris Maginnis, Fred Simkins, Alan Sharkey, Col Clinton Riley, Col Barry Paddison. Thanks to Derick Bostridge and Peter King for their adaptation of *Hurstpierpoint College 1849–1995*, published by Phillimore.

Special thanks go to Major Kevin Glenn (Rtd), my former Group Commander – who persuaded me to write this book – and also Shaun Barrington of The History Press for publishing it.

Thanks also to my wife Fiona and children, Isabella, Angelina and Jamie for their patience and understanding during my time away interviewing, photographing and researching for this book.

Picture Credits

Rita Boswell and Derick Bostridge for all their fantastic CCF photos. Graham Atwell, Andy Axten, Matt Hedgecoe, Mike Nolan, Dan Fox and Chris Young for the use of their ACF photos. AAC, ACF, ACFA, MoD, RCAC, Avpro Picture Library, Imperial War Museum and the Australian War Museum.

Cadet Patrons

On behalf of all the Cadets and Adult Instructors in my Detachment, a personal thank you to the following individuals and organisations for supporting us in our numerous and varied activities and endeavours: Samuel Botchey, Jack Petchey, Andrew Wallington-Smith, Harrow Youth Opportunity Fund, Jack Petchey Foundation and The Society of Apothecaries. Your kindness is greatly appreciated by all concerned.

Photographs

I have sought to provide a balanced view of the Army Cadet Force by means of suitable photos from each period of its history. As you can probably imagine, it has been difficult to find pictures of cadets taken in the 19th century as so few exist. To those people who kindly loaned their personal photos, I am extremely grateful, as some images say more about their respective period than I could ever describe in words. I have used every photo that I have been able to get hold of that portrays any aspect of either the Army Cadet Force or the CCF in their early days. I make no apology for this, as many of these photos have never been published. For me these are real gems that reflect the impressive longevity of the ACF and CCF.

Today virtually every cadet and adult instructor has either a camera or mobile phone that is capable of image capture. So therefore every ACF activity, event, exercise or parade can be displayed for all to see. It would have been the easiest thing in the world for me simply to use all my own photos and those that appear on the numerous excellent ACF websites. However, that would be doing a disservice to all those who have served in the past, as their stories, events and parades need to be appreciated also, it is only through the hard work and dedication of those that have gone before that we have an organisation that is the envy of many; and the 150th anniversary celebrations give us a rare window of opportunity to look back in print.

Virtually no cadet or adult instructor had a camera even a hundred years ago, so most photographic records of a major event were produced by a local newspaper or an official military representative. There were of course some exceptions, but they were few and far between. Also, for some strange and inexplicable reason, we in the UK were slow to appreciate the value of keeping a detailed photographic record, in comparison with other countries who formed their own model of the Army Cadet Force.

For example, at the Imperial War Museum, the keepers of our military heritage, in their entire photographic collection – millions of images – only two of the Army Cadet Force are catalogued! But that cannot be the sum total actually taken, which begs the question, where are the others?

Author's Appeal

There must of course be thousands of Army Cadet Force photos out there, long forgotten and now lying hidden away in dusty old envelopes within official archives, or stored away in former ACF members' attics just waiting to be discovered.

If you have in your possession photos of cadets taken in an era long gone and want to see them either published or displayed for posterity, then please kindly post either the original photo or a copy, which can be in the form of a CD, to Mike Ryan, C/O The History Press, The Mill, Brimscombe Port, Stroud, Gloucestershire, GL5 2QG. – giving as much information about its provenance as possible so that I can accurately log all the details.

As a member of the British Commission for Military History, it is my intention to set up a website dedicated to preserving the history of the Army Cadet Force, so that all may enjoy it – and with your kind help I am sure that this will be possible.

Thank you in advance.

Mike Ryan

ABBREVIATIONS

AAC – Australian Army Cadets
ACF – Army Cadet Force
ACFA – Army Cadet Force Association
BNCA – British National Cadet Association
CCAT – Combined Cadet Adventure Training
CCF – Combined Cadet Force
CFAV – Cadet Force Adult Volunteer
CTC – Cadet Training Centre
DET – Detachment
EASP – Exercise Action Safety Plan
OTC – Officer Training Corps
RA – Risk Assessment
RAMC – Royal Army Medical Corps
RASP – Range Action Safety Plan
RCAC – Royal Canadian Army Cadets
SAS – Special Air Service

ACF DETACHMENTS

Scotland
1st BN The Highlanders ACF
2nd BN The Highlanders ACF
Angus and Dundee BN ACF
Argyll and Sutherland Highlanders BN ACF
Black Watch BN ACF
Orkney Independent Cadet Battery ACF
Shetland Independent Cadet Battery ACF
Glasgow and Lanarkshire BN ACF
Lothian and Borders BN AC
The West Lowland BN ACF

North East
Cleveland ACF
Durham ACF
Northumbria ACF

North West
Cheshire ACF
Cumbria ACF
Greater Manchester ACF
Isle of Man ACF
Lancashire ACF
Merseyside ACF

Yorks & Humberside
Humberside and South Yorkshire ACF
Yorkshire (N&W) ACF

Wales
Dyfed & Glamorgan ACF
Clwyd & Gwynedd ACF
Gwent & Powys ACF

West Midlands
Hereford and Worcester ACF
Shropshire ACF
Staffordshire and West Midland North Sector ACF
Warwickshire and West Midlands South Sector ACF

East Midlands
Derbyshire ACF
Leicestershire, Northamptonshire and Rutland ACF
Lincolnshire ACF
Nottinghamshire ACF

South West
The City and County of Bristol ACF
The Cornwall Cadet BN (LI) ACF
Devon ACF
Dorset ACF
The Gloucestershire Cadet BN (ACF)
Somerset Cadet BN (ACF) LI
Wiltshire ACF

South East
Buckinghamshire ACF
Hampshire and Isle of Wight ACF
Kent ACF
Oxfordshire ACF
Royal County of Berkshire ACF
Surrey ACF
Sussex ACF

London
City of London and North East Sector ACF
Middlesex and North West London ACF
London South East Sector ACF
Greater London South West Sector ACF

East
Essex ACF
Bedfordshire ACF
Cambridgeshire ACF
Hertfordshire ACF
Norfolk ACF
Suffolk ACF

Northern Ireland
1st Northern Ireland Battalion ACF
2nd Northern Ireland Battalion ACF

PREFACE

Mention the words Army Cadet Force to most people, and they will probably throw you a blank look, because they do not know anything about it; or they have heard of it, but know very little. This lack of knowledge is not too hard to understand, as little or nothing has been written in any detail about this organisation. It is almost as if someone wants to keep what it gets up to secret. But what a well-kept secret, as the Army Cadet Force has been around in one guise or another since 1859, which makes it the UK's oldest youth organisation, perhaps the world's.

In 2010, it celebrates its 150th Anniversary, and everyone within the Army Cadet Force will certainly be doing their level best to make sure that we commemorate this event in a spectacular manner and with as high a profile as possible. At a time of constant media coverage that seems always to be dinning into us how our youth are failing both us and themselves, a lot of people are going to be shocked to learn that not all young people are hooded thugs who roam our towns and cities looking for trouble. Indeed, contrary to popular belief, the vast majority of our teenagers are utterly decent young people who have ambition, compassion and a sense of purpose to their lives. I should know, because for the past fifteen years I have had the honour and privilege of working with thousands of them. I am an author and broadcaster, but I am just as proud and happy to be an Officer and an Instructor in the Army Cadet Force. In writing this book, I hope to show people what it is that we do and why we have been so successful in helping hundreds of thousands of young people over the years by living true to our motto, 'inspire, to achieve'.

THE CHARTER OF THE ARMY CADET FORCE

The Army Cadet Force is a national voluntary youth organisation. It is sponsored by the MoD. Its aim is to inspire young people to achieve success in life with a spirit of service to the Queen, their country and their local community, and to develop in them the qualities required of a good citizen. This aim is achieved by:

A. Providing progressive cadet training, often of a challenging and exciting nature, to foster confidence, self reliance, initiative, loyalty, and a sense of service to other people.

B. Encouraging the development of personal powers of practical leadership and the ability to work successfully as a member of a team.

C. Stimulating an interest in the Army, its achievements, skills and values.

D. Advising and preparing those considering a career in the services or with the reserve forces.

I

INTRODUCTION

The Army Cadet Force can trace its history back to 1859 and owes its existence to the French. Were it not for their ambition to invade England, there would have been no need for additional manpower to be called-up and therefore no need to recruit young boys and men as members of a hastily assembled militia.

During this period the British army and navy were both so heavily committed to supporting the empire in India – following the Indian Mutiny, or First War of Independence, of 1857 – that it was felt that with so much of our military might involved both there and elsewhere around the world, we were seriously vulnerable to a surprise attack and the real possibility of French occupation.

This threat of course was nothing new, as we had been fighting our European neighbours on and off for centuries. The difference this time was that the French Army on our doorstep, under the ambitious leadership of Napoleon III, was on the increase, while our own home-based forces were shrinking. The spark for a sudden rise in tensions was an assassination attempt on Napoleon III on 14 January 1858. It transpired that the would be assassin was an Italian by the name of Felice Orsini, and that the bombs that he had manufactured for use in the attack had been made in England – which led some senior French military officers to believe that the British were fully complicit in the attempt, and that they needed to be taught a lesson. Deciding that something had to be done quickly to counter this perceived threat, the government began a massive building programme. Large forts and defensive positions were constructed in and around possible landing sites and ports. In addition, on 12 May 1859, the Secretary of State sent out an open letter inviting the formation of a Volunteer Corps.

Up and down the country, many answered the call and within a relatively short period of time some 100,000 men were enrolled as volunteers. Although nobody could have predicted it at the time, this Corps in one guise or another would eventually evolve into the Territorial Army.

1. A somewhat exaggerated image depicting an invasion of England in 1805.

2. Octavia Hill. A remarkable woman who campaigned relentlessly to achieve her aims.

3. A postcard from Octavia Hill mentioning cadets.

4. The Octavia Hill plaque in Southwark, London.

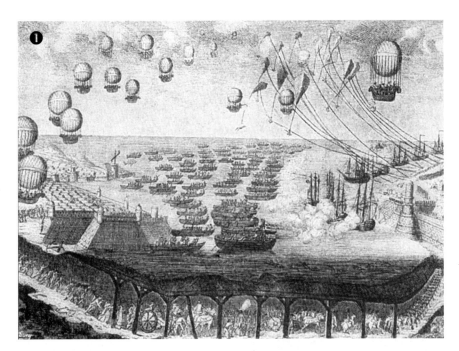

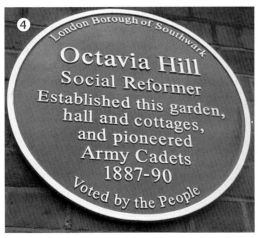

5. The Zulu War was fascinating for young boys and acted as something of a recruiting Sergeant. This image from The Illustrated London News depicts action during the first major battle of the war, at Isandlwana on 22 January 1879.

6. British Boy Soldiers embarking for the Napoleonic Wars.

7. Cadets from the 1879 renactment group recreate R.E. Fripps' famous Isandlwana painting.

8. Surrey Volunteer Corps. The Surrey Rifle Volunteers were established in 1859 to face the apparent threat of invasion by France. In 1882, four of the eight existing Corps were allocated to the Queen's and four to the East Surrey Regiment. In 1908 the Volunteers would become the Territorial Force.

9. Two young cadets pose for a portrait in cadet uniform, rather than their normal school attire. Choosing to be photographed in uniform was common, not surprisingly in view of the sumptuous attire.

Jawaharlal Nehru, future Indian Prime Minister, wearing the uniform of the Harrow Rifles.

Officers and cadets from Harrow School forming ranks prior to a major review.

OTC cadets form up for a photo during a school open day.

The volunteers were all provided with free weapons by the Government, but had to pay for their uniforms and equipment out of their own pockets. This of course led to a great variation in standards, as some volunteers had more money to spend on their kit than others, so something of a two-tier force developed.

**WAR OFFICE, PALL MALL,
MAY 12, 1859**

Her Majesty's Lieutenant for the county of......

Her Majesty's Government having had under consideration the propriety of permitting the formation of volunteer rifle corps, under the Act of 44 George III., cap. 54, as well as artillery corps and companies in maritime towns in which there may be forts and batteries, I have the honour to inform you that I shall be prepared to receive through you, and consider any proposal with that object, which may emanate from the county under your charge.

The principal and most important provisions of the act are -

That the corps be formed under officers bearing the commission of the Lieutenant of the county.
That its members must take the Oath of Allegiance before a Deputy Lieutenant or justice of the Peace, or a commissioned officer of the corps.
That it be liable to be called out in case of actual invasion, or appearance of an enemy in force on the coast, or in case of rebellion arising out of either of those emergencies.
That while thus under arms its members are subject to military law, and entitled to be billeted and to receive pay in like manner as the regular army.
That all commissioned officers disabled in actual service are entitled to half pay, and non-commissioned officers and privates to the benefit of the Chelsea Hospital, and widows of commissioned officers killed in service to such pensions for life as are given to widows of officers of Her Majesty's regular forces ...

The conditions on which Her Majesty's Government will recommend to Her Majesty the acceptance of any proposal are -
That the formation of the corps be recommended by the Lord-Lieutenant of the county.
That the corps be subject to the provisions of the Act already quoted.
That its members undertake to provide their own arms and equipments, and to defray all expenses attending the corps, except in the event of its being assembled for actual service.

Harrow Volunteer Rifle Corps shooting team, 1904.

That the rules and regulations which may be thought necessary be submitted to me, in accordance with the 56th section of the Act.

The uniform and equipments of the corps may be settled by the members, subject to your approval, but the arms though provided at the expense of the members, must be furnished under the superintendence and according to the regulations of this department, in order to secure a perfect uniformity of gauge.

The establishment of offices and non-commissioned officers will be fixed by me; and recorded in books of this office; and, in order that I may be enabled to determine the proportion, you will be pleased to specify the number of private men, which you will recommend, and into how many companies you propose to divide them.

I have only to add that I shall look to you, as Her Majesty's Lieutenant, for the nomination of proper persons to be appointed officers, subject to the Queen's approval. I have the honour to be, your most obedient servant.

J. PEEL

Initially the volunteers operated quite autonomously, but over time they became more integrated within the existing framework of the British Army's order of battle – making them an extremely valuable asset. At about the same time a number of boys' schools also formed their own Volunteer Corps, the earliest ones at Eton, Felsted, Harrow, Hurstpierpoint, Marlborough, Rossall, Rugby and Winchester. The School Volunteer Corps was open to senior boys and schoolmasters only, and had a role not dissimilar to that performed by Home Guard school units formed in 1940. These school-based units would eventually become the Combined Cadet Force (CCF).

The school-based extension of the Volunteer Corps would have surprised no one; it must be remembered that during the 18th century young boys serving in the armed forces was far from unusual. Boys performed many roles, ranging from that of drummer and fifer to more demanding positions that often involved them leading men who were far older than they were. This might seem odd, but in those days an Army officer's commission was bought rather than earned, which meant that if you were from a financially well off family you could buy your way up through the army's ranks. This is how General James Wolfe started his illustrious military career. Having joined the army at the grand old age of thirteen, he worked his way up to become one of England's greatest military commanders. Apart from the very occasional exception, if you were rich you became an officer, poor and you joined the ranks as a common soldier. I mention this as in due course this distinction would have some bearing on the evolution of the cadet forces.

For the regular army, the School Volunteer Corps was clearly a wonderful concept, as it provided the Crown forces with a constant stream of well educated young gentlemen who were also well disciplined and proficient in military skills. If any army has the ability to tap into such a rich vein of officer recruits as a matter of routine, a mindset will start to develop that is hard to change or influence. And it is an attitude that can easily backfire.

Although this point is particularly relevant to the Army, it also applies to the British government. For they had built up their entire argument for more defences, more soldiers and of course the formation of the Volunteer Corps under the threat of a French invasion. When this threat diminished, people quite rightly began to question what was going on, recalling that the French had been our allies in the Crimean War of 1855 and since then had shown no evidence of potential aggression whatsoever, such as significant military build-ups at their channel coastal ports. Indeed, they were preoccupied elsewhere, heavily engaged in a bloody war with Austria. When in 1870 the French were defeated by the Prussians, the game was truly up for the advocates of strong homeland defence, as there simply could not be an invasion – France had no possible means of mounting one. This of course set the alarm bells ringing for both the British Army and the Volunteer Corps, as they feared that all they had built up over the years would be dismantled and lost.

They need not have worried, as the military and political 'spin doctors' of the day came up with a new line. If the Prussians could defeat the French, then they

OTC cadets forming ranks in advance of an exercise.

Senior Army officers and dignitaries take the salute from cadets during a major review in Southern England.

must be the new threat, and therefore we risked invasion from them! People who have an interest in both British history and the cadet forces have often wondered why the schools units of the day survived when there was no real obvious military purpose for them after 1870. This is why.

Young cadets proudly show off a trophy following a house competition.

Hurstpierpoint Cadet Corps, 1899.

The First Hurst VIII to shoot at Bisley, 15 July 1897.

'Splendid turnout Sergeant – keep it up.'

The Grand Review of the Volunteer Rifle Corps by Her Majesty the Queen, 1860. (Courtesy of London Metropolitan Archives.)

OTC cadets marching out for weekend manoeuvres.

The Mafeking Cadet Corps

The Mafeking Cadet Corps has a particularly significant place in the history of the development of the ACF. This group of young boys saw action during the siege of Mafeking at the height of the Second Boer War in 1899–1900. The idea for the creation of such a Corps came from its founder Colonel Robert Baden-Powell, a man who had immense belief and confidence in young people. As a young man growing up in England, he had seen cadets working alongside both regular soldiers and militia and felt that they had much to offer.

During the siege, Colonel Baden-Powell was the commander of all forces in the besieged town and really faced a terrible struggle against the formidable Boers who surrounded him. For many in the town, the situation at first appeared hopeless as the Boers had more men and more capable artillery than the British. Baden-Powell refused to capitulate, and set about devising a number of ruses he hoped would deceive the enemy. One of his first actions was to send soldiers out to plant fence posts along the lines of possible enemy advance. At first his soldiers thought he was mad, as they had no barbed wire to string between them. But they quickly realised what he was trying to do. To the distant Boers, it would appear that this area was going to be difficult to attack as it was apparently covered in razor wire, forcing them to look elsewhere for an easier infiltration route. Elsewhere, the defenders set about digging holes in the ground, to give the impression that they were planting mines. In reality of course there were none.

However from the Army Cadet Force's point of view, Baden-Powell's best decision was the formation of the Mafeking Cadet Corps. Realising that he had only limited manpower at his disposal, he decided to use the enthusiasm and tenacity of his young followers to his advantage. Typical roles they performed

A comtemporary sketch of a cadet taking orders at Mafeking.

The famous Mafeking blue stamp.

Top right, with apologies for the quality of the image but this is the only known picture of the Mafeking Cadets. They are all wearing Glengarry caps.

included carrying messages, moving casualties, spotting enemy troop movements and helping out in the hospital. This valuable work helped free up soldiers for frontline duties. The cadets themselves consisted of volunteer white boys below fighting age. The most remarkable thing about the Corps was the fact that their leader, Sergeant-Major Warner Goodyear, was only 13 years old. Uniform consisted of a Khaki jacket and usually a wide-brimmed hat, which was worn one side up, or a Glengarry cap.

The Corps evoked pride and admiration amongst the general population of Mafeking and helped take their minds off the siege, which was no mean feat, as it lasted for 217 days. The sight of young cadets darting from the town to the outlying forts with orders from HQ became something of a regular sight. At first they used donkeys, but these were eventually eaten, forcing them to take to bicycles instead. From the civilian's point of view, the most useful role of the cadets was spotting the Boers' siege guns and which direction they were pointed. Once this was known people could move out of the line of fire.

On one occasion Baden-Powell stopped one of the cadets who had just ridden through a heavy barrage and said 'You will get hit one of these days riding about like that when shells are flying'. The cadet replied 'I pedal so quick, Sir, they'd never catch me.' During the siege one young boy, Frankie Brown aged nine, was killed by a shell and cited as the first cadet casualty. Though the official line was that boys in the Corps had to be aged 11 or over before they could be enrolled on the nominal role book. One fact not in dispute however, is the bravery of the young boys. In all, 38 Cadets were awarded the Defence of Mafeking bar, which was mounted on the Queen's South Africa Medal. The story of the Mafeking Cadet Corps did much to inspire young boys in England to join their local Cadet unit. Their success was also noted by the British military hierarchy.

I

CADET BEGINNINGS

It was around this time that the word cadet began to appear more frequently in English. The term was generally used to refer to young boys serving with the School Volunteer Corps, but it also began to be used describing boys serving alongside the men in the Volunteer Corps. The word itself is of French origin, and means little chief, but can also be used simply to mean a young boy. It is probable that young boys who had any form of connection to the military in France were called 'cadets' – and because of the close proximity of Britain, the name jumped across the Channel. Of course a considerable part of the British Army's military jargon and terminology originated from the French, 'lieutenant' for example (one who acts in place of another), or platoon (*peloton*).

Outside the School Volunteer Corps, the adult volunteer battalions began to raise their own cadet companies, generally recruited on a district or county basis. Often they were simply made up of sons or younger relatives of those already serving – usually a good recruiting source – but increasingly, complete 'outsiders' began to join up who had no prior connection either to the Volunteer Corps or the Army.

In May 1860, the Cadet companies received a major boost to their credibility when 35 cadets were invited to march past Queen Victoria. This was a tremendous honour for them, as not only were they representing their fellow cadets, they were also leading the Queen's Westminster Rifle Volunteers who were participating, like them, in the first Volunteers review, held in London's Hyde Park. This event was not an isolated one, as many similar reviews took place throughout Britain that year.

O.T.C Camp Tidworth Park

Publications of the period such as the *Boy's Own Paper* reveal some interesting information concerning what weapons and equipment the Cadet Corps was equipped with. They mention the fact that the cadets were often led by both fife and drums during the reviews and that they were armed with ex-Royal Irish Constabulary rifles. The cadets were supervised and trained by officers and sergeants of the regiment they were attached to, fostering that close knit military family type environment that always characterised the British regimental system.

To join a cadet company an entrance fee and a subscription was required. So rapid was the growth of the Cadet Corps during this period through its own momentum, it was felt necessary in the 1863 edition of the Volunteers Regulations to confirm the fact that their formation was now officially authorised and that they would be supported. This rubber stamp of approval was extremely important as it meant that the cadets were now allowed to wear the same uniform as their parent battalion and were secure in the knowledge that they would be both officered and administered by them. As with the Volunteers, uniform varied immensely from district to district and was dependent on money available and the style, or lack of it, of their officers.

The Cadet Corps was basically a means of feeding the Volunteers and regular Army with recruits, but there were many at the time who realised that if the cadet movement was to survive in the long term, it must have broader appeal outside the military. Fortunately for the Cadet Corps (if no one else) England was beset by serious social problems, most of which were the by-products of the Industrial Revolution: bad housing, alcoholism, poor diet, high crime rates and appalling work conditions. Some of it sounds familiar.

There were many in Victorian times who cared passionately about the welfare of the poor, and did much to publicise their plight by means of constant campaigning. They were particularly sympathetic to the cause of the young. The social reformers saw in the Cadet Corps an organisation that potentially offered much in their attempts to rescue young boys from both mental and physical stagnation. One of the leading social reformers of the day was Octavia Hill, whose main area of work was concerned with poor housing in South-East London. Apart from her pioneering social work, Octavia Hill was also a champion of the National Trust and did a great deal to help establish that wonderful organisation. She is also without doubt one of the key figures in the development of the Cadet Corps, as it was through her drive and determination that a unit was formed in a slum district of London.

Her motives however were not militaristic. It was simply the case that she knew young boys were likely to be attracted to a uniformed organisation that was connected to the Army. The alternative, the standard social reformer's package, involved a modus operandi that was, to put it bluntly, a turn-off to the young, on account of its jaded and outdated 'poorhouse', evangelising methods.

That is not to say that the Cadet Corps was perfect. Indeed, Octavia Hill quickly recognised that some fundamental changes had to take place within the Cadet Corps for it to survive. She was seriously concerned about the fact that the Cadet

Cadets marching into Tidworth Park.

An early reminder that the ACF and CCF were and are not the only cadet organisations in the world: see chapter VII, page 113. Cadets being inspected on Empire day in 1939, location Nairobi, Kenya.

Cadets practise sending signals.

Corps was under the control of the newly formed Territorial Force Association, and strongly felt that it should be independent of it because the TFA's primary purpose was, understandably enough, to support the reserve forces, rather than to offer social and educational welfare. It became apparent to her that once the military need for new recruits and reserves reduced during times of peace, the Cadet Corps would be vulnerable to disbandment. What she wanted for the Cadet Corps was autonomy, and the ability to adapt into a more forward-thinking organisation that would be effective and demonstrably of value during times of war *and* peace. It was through Octavia Hill's tireless efforts that an independent detachment was set up in Southwark – one that is still in existence to this day. Not only did she help form this unit, she was also instrumental in securing money, staff and even uniforms for it. The uniforms were acquired from Eton school.

It should be borne in mind that Octavia Hill was not the only person to see merit in the Cadet Corps, as there were many other advocates up and down the country who also clearly saw the benefits of such an organisation within their own communities. The city of Manchester, for example, can lay claim to be amongst the first to have a self-administered battalion for boys. This was formed in 1884 by A. P. Ledward under the designation of the 1st Cadet Battalion the Manchester Regiment. When first sanctioned, this unit had an initial strength of three officers and some forty cadets; by 1900 its numbers had risen to an amazing six hundred all ranks.

Meanwhile back in London, things were about to change. In 1885 an East London Cadet Corps was formed in Toynbee Hall in Whitechapel, which in turn prompted the establishment of a number of other cadet companies, these usually sponsored by public schools. The 1890 Army List acknowledges the existence of no less than forty units.

Harrow cadets form a Guard of Honour as King George V arrives at their school.

The three key areas for the Cadet Corps units were Birmingham, London and Manchester. By the 1890s, the expansion of the Cadet Corps was rapid, with many prominent figures of the day actively promoting its activities. The people involved were of no particular type, and included soldiers, politicians, social reformers and even clergymen, who formed Cadet Companies as an extension of their normal parish activities. Something it is difficult to imagine happening today.

The language of the day when describing cadets was interesting. During one particular meeting held at Paddington on 20 February 1893, Lord Methuen, GOC Home District, General Sir George White, V.C. C-in-C Yeomanry and Volunteers and the Bishop of Marlborough were present. The Commander-in-Chief is reported as

Hurstpierpoint College contingent marching into Tidworth Park.

saying that he 'accepted the brilliant results reported to them that night, and was much pleased with the specimens of the Cadet Corps now before him.' Referring to young people as 'specimens' would not find favour in some quarters today. The reaction doesn't bear thinking about. The rest of his report is extremely positive and gives an insight into just how favourably the Cadet Corps was viewed:

> Inasmuch as the importance and value of any social movement (eg the temperance cause) was intensified and accentuated by the misery and unhappiness caused by indulgence in unrestrained liberty and abuse of freedom, so the widespread anarchy and lawlessness that marked much of the life in the large centres of population today must intensify and accentuate the value of a movement such as that of a Volunteer Cadet Corps.

He considered that 'these boys of England were the most enterprising spirits in the world ... Enrolled in these corps, they were a band of hope for the Empire.' Besides the social benefit of this movement, there was, of course, another. The young boys who first joined the Cadet Corps and afterwards enlisted would prove as useful a boost to the Army as did the one-year volunteers in Germany. They learnt the first duty of citizenship, namely, the duty of defending the land that gave them birth. For Britain, he observed, there was the first line of defence, the Navy; the second line, the Army; the third line, that grand and essentially English force, the Volunteers; and he would add a fourth line, the Cadet Corps.

He did not think, furthermore, that the boys he saw before him would be found among those who on Sundays were seen desecrating the lions in Trafalgar Square by using their backs as a platform from which to cry down anything that did not suit their own views! Rather, their training as Volunteer cadets would induce them to raise their eyes to the statue of that noble Englishman whose last signal was 'England expects every man to do his duty.' The devotion of a few good men and kind women was already doing wonders for working lads. And he appealed to the parents of England to extend their sympathy to this movement so that its members might grow up true and useful men.

OTC at Bisley 1927.

The South African War naturally led to increased activity both within the Volunteer Corps and the Cadet Corps. For instance, within the school Cadet Corps units the number of cadet contingents increased from 41 in 1898 to 99 in 1902. All cadet

units around this time enjoyed an increase in their roll, a common phenomenon during periods of crisis. Basically, everyone wanted to play their part. The King's Royal Rifle Corps even sent a contingent to South Africa as part of the City Imperial Volunteers, a deployment that won them a battle honour. They are in fact the only cadet unit to have such an award. The Boer War had a huge effect on the British Army and indeed the reserve forces back in England. It was quickly realised that the Volunteer Corps role had to change. Instead of a defence against invasion, it would become an expeditionary force, and therefore a name change was required. The Volunteers would now be known as the Territorial Force. The changes were advocated by Lord Haldane, and they of course meant change for the Cadet Corps.

Prior to the announcement, the Cadet Corps' role was in need of clarification. During this time the difference between the Cadet Corps as a training organisation and the Volunteer Battalions as potential combatants was by no means clearly defined or understood. For example, prior to 1907, boys over 17 could potentially join their parent Volunteer battalion and train with the adults, while still remaining in the Cadet Corps. This unusual situation was also allowed during the Second World War with the Home Guard. Working so closely helped forge strong ties between the cadets and adults – making training and recruitment much easier for all concerned.

Within the school-based units, change was also in the air. In 1889, a camp was held at Churn Downs that involved 11 officers, six sergeant instructors and 204 cadets from Bedford, Bradfield, Haileybury and Sherborne public schools. The camp was a significant event for many reasons, not least because of a mock battle held in Aldershot in honour of the German Emperor Wilhelm II. He later said he had been extremely impressed with what he had seen. The event of course did the school-based units a lot of good and helped create the impetus for further development and recruitment.

In 1906 a War Office Committee was formed to consider the chronic shortage of officers for both the regular and reserve forces. Its findings recommended that an Officers Training Corps (OTC) be formed in two divisions, a senior one for universities and a junior one for schools. Any school that could produce a minimum of one officer and thirty cadets could form a contingent, and a hundred did so immediately. In most cases these OTCs were merely replacing existing cadet corps units.

The junior element of the OTC did not stay the course with its original name and would evolve into what is now the Combined Cadet Force (CCF). It was also around this time of reform that the term 'Cadet Force' came into use. This coincided with the handover of units to the newly formed Territorial Associations in 1910.

Following this reorganisation, the cadet forces continued to expand at a steady rate; rising from 14,399 in 1911 to 41,108 in 1913, and then 105,121 in 1918, to a peak of 119,706 in 1921. The figures spike spectacularly, and unsurprisingly, around the Great War, the numbers further swelled by the affiliation of the Boys' and Church Lads' Brigades. These figures are all the more impressive when you

OTC cadets clearing out their tents for a hygiene inspection.

Young cadets armed with rifles and ammunition bandoliers pose for a school OTC portrait.

Young cadets enjoying an annual camp in 1911.

remember that many young teenagers fought as boy soldiers as part of the regular army, or joined the scout movement, which in those days actively trained with weapons as part of a homeland defence strategy.

The cadet forces during this period were in a very strong position, as not only did they produce good young citizens, they also produced first-rate soldiers. Their value was officially endorsed when in 1917 the Public and Secondary Schools Cadet Association was formed with the sole remit of looking after the interests of school units in the Army Cadet Force.

After reading this, you might think the Army Cadet Force's long-term future would have been secure. But you would be wrong. The unimaginable cost of the War and then the 1929 Wall Street Crash left pretty much everything insecure. There was little money around to support anybody or anything and that included the Army Cadet Force.

The War Office ceased to support and administer it directly, and instead passed it over to the Council of County Territorial Associations – with a paltry annual grant of £750. Although this decision had been expected, its outcome and implications had not. The infamous defence cut-backs that occurred in 1923 became known as Geddes' Axe. With little money and direct support now available, many units

closed up and down the country. By 1928, cadet numbers had dropped to less than 50,000 in 949 active companies. Worse was yet to come.

Shirt sleeve order at camp in Tidworth Park.

In 1930 all official recognition, arms and funding was withdrawn. This, coupled with a number of educational authorities banning cadets from schools, led to a dramatic decline in both cadet numbers and units. Only the most established survived. Urgent action was needed to restore the reputation of the cadet forces. Thus the British National Cadet Association (BNCA) was formed under Field-Marshal Lord Allenby, with the Prince of Wales as Patron.

Its mission was extremely successful in raising the profile of the cadets once again, so much so that the decision was taken to remove the Cadet Force from the remit of the Council of County Territorial Associations and give the BNCA autonomy. Initially there was no funding for either the BNCA or the cadets themselves, until in 1937 it was agreed that a grant of five shillings would be paid for every cadet that fulfilled certain criteria.

Although this was better than nothing, the cadet forces were still not faring as well as their OTC counterparts, who had the specific remit of producing potential officer candidates. This difference in fortunes stems from the fact that the OTC operated in the shadows and off the political radar, while the Army Cadet Force had to constantly seek publicity and high profile advocates to state its case – simply in order to survive. As a result the OTC's path forward was much smoother than that of its brother organisation: Army Cadet Force strength in 1939 – 20,000; Officer Training Corps strength 1939 – 30,000. In order for the Army Cadet Force to regain its former vigour, it needed a war. In 1939 it got one.

Victoria College
Jersey OTC
1909.

The King visiting
Jersey OTC.

Harrow Rifles in camp in 1911. How many of these young men would perish in the war to end all wars?

❸

1. Prior to the introduction of radios, cadets used flags, mirrors, signal lanterns and even fireworks as a means of signalling.

2. College shooting team 1906.

3. Cadets from a cycle section prepare for an inspection.

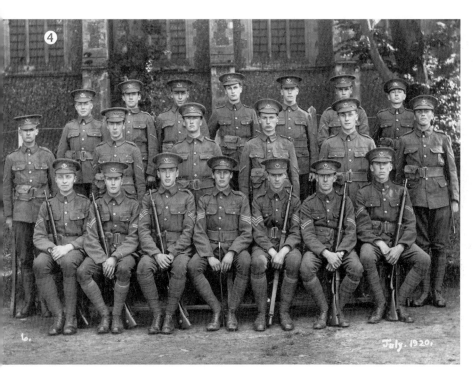

1. A rare photograph showing cadets using a Lewis gun during a fire and manoeuvre exercise.

2. Band competition, Tidworth camp 1935.

3. Band practice on a cold and misty morning.

4. Cadet NCOs, July 1920.

Cadets
demonstrate a
Lee Enfield Rifle
tripod mount.

Cadets take
cover during an
anti-ambush
exercise.

Cadets pose for
an unusually
informal photo,
late nineteenth
century.

1. Cadet numbers plummeted after the end of the Great War but the OTCs never disappeared.

2. Harrow's bugle band.

3. Harrow Rifles forming square, including a young W. Churchill. We can't find him either.

1. Australian cadets at Bisley, looking rather like Union troops of the American Civil War.

2. King George V inspecting Harrow Rifle Corps.

3. Now where did that little chap get to? OTC escape and evasion exercise.

4. OTC cadets pose for a team photo after winning a competition.

July 1914.

OTC cadets at the outbreak of the First World War.

OTC cadets at the railway station with rifles, probably some time after the First World War. Something that would not be seen today, of course.

An extremely rare portrait studio photograph of a young cadet in service dress taken during the First World War.

OTC Drum
Major.

OTC Drummer
Boy.

**OTC NCOs
1909.**

This is where most of the men photographed above would go five years later. Despite the fact that the BEF was ill-prepared for the continental, industrial war it faced, it is impossible to argue that the OTC did not contribute to its early genuine successes and the eventual victory.

Senior OTC cadets at the outbreak of the First World War. In August 1914 there were about 28,000 officers in the British Army, more than half in the reserves. By the war's end nearly 250,000 had been commissioned. The need was immense.

Young signallers after a communications exercise in Sussex.

1. Australian cadets at Bisley, 1911.

2. Australian cadets impress the townsfolk of Brighton.

3. Recruiting poster from the 1940s.

II

FINEST HOUR

The Second World War was probably the most extraordinary time to have been a cadet. One could guess this to be so. The threat of invasion had returned, so all hands were needed – including those of young army cadets. This was no vague and distant threat, as the Germans had already swept all before them in Europe by means of their *Blitzkrieg* tactics (Lightning War). It appeared that nobody could stop them. That is apart from the occupiers of one tiny nation between the European mainland and the United States.

Adolf Hitler of course realised that invading Britain would be no easy task, so he put together a team of his best military advisers. For the invasion phase to succeed, two things had to happen first; The RAF had to be shot out of the skies or preferably bombed before it got airborne, while the Royal Navy's fleet of warships had to be either sunk or denied access to the English Channel. Then, and only then, would an invasion fleet have a chance of landing.

At the start of the Second World War, the various cadet forces were extremely small and relatively poorly equipped. That situation changed rapidly, when the real possibility of an invasion dawned on everyone. There was a perceived problem that would be overcome. With so much of Britain's armed forces involved in fighting in Europe, there were very few officers and sergeant instructors left behind who could be spared to run and train cadet detachments. Every able-bodied man was needed either for the regular services or the reserve forces. This meant that the officers and instructors that were assigned to support the cadets were either medically unfit for service through injury or age or they were employed in a reserve occupation that excluded them from active service. But this did not mean they were not competent or of value to the cadets. Indeed, in most cases they most certainly were, as many had fought during the First World War or on a battlefield elsewhere in the Empire – which gave them knowledge and experience – and given a chance to play their part in this war, no doubt they grasped it with both hands.

Cadets did an enormous amount of work behind the scenes preparing our armed forces' equipment for D-Day.

58

Cadets spent hours during the Second World War studying official information posters, to be as current as possible with their knowledge.

One of the first jobs tasked to the cadets was digging long, shallow trenches across possible glider landing sites. This meant digging up rugby and football playing fields all across the country, especially those located near to strategic locations. Observation points were also set up along the coast to help the regular army in looking out for enemy activity. Often, cadets would strike up friendships with the soldiers assigned to their local districts. This at times led to them running errands or delivering low-priority messages. In return, the soldiers frequently gave them military training lessons or provided instruction on how to handle and use personal weaponry. There was no set curriculum for this type of training; it was simply a case of getting hold of whatever was available at the time.

Throughout the summer of 1940, Spitfires and Hurricanes spiralled high above the Garden of England as they jousted with the Luftwaffe. Far below them cadets were frequently used to spot where stray bombs had been dropped or to help in finding crash sites of friend or foe. Cadets also played a significant role during the Blitz, often helping to clear houses and roads of rubble after bombing raids. This was not all, as I have been told stories of cadets helping to entertain young children during bombing raids as they hid in London's underground tube stations, which doubled as air raid shelters.

There were concerns in the War Office about just what type of involvement the cadets could have in helping the armed forces – especially if an invasion did take place. The concern was how the Germans would view them. Would they be classed as prisoners of war? The Germans of course knew of the British cadets, as they had seen them train and march during peacetime events organised to create better relations between the two countries.

The official War Office line was that cadets were not to be used in any direct combat role, but could assist regular and reserve forces in low-threat areas. In the event of an invasion, they were to stay at home. It was of course a blurred line, often stepped over at the discretion of local commanders. From the Army's point of view, they certainly wanted to encourage the older boys to enlist and frequently took them away on regular training camps to show them, as far as possible, what they faced, should they join up.

A more enjoyable role for the cadets was playing the enemy during military training exercises – a task all cadets both then and now love. There were also unofficial benefits to be had from associating with the troops, as it could bring a few extra luxuries that were probably not available at home.

The War naturally stimulated considerable growth in the cadet forces, just as had happened during the Boer War and the Great War. This was great news for the BNCA. The conflict was a superb recruiting sergeant and was doing the BNCA's job for them. By 1941, all boys and girls aged sixteen or over were expected to join a youth organisation that could help in the war effort. This was not compulsory.

In 1942, the War Office decided that it would like to support the cadet forces once again, and assumed the responsibility from the BCNA of supplying weapons, accommodation and equipment. The BCNA retained its articles of association, just in case the War Office withdrew suddenly, as it had done before. Although reduced in its responsibilities, the Association continued to deal with sports matters, welfare, publications and general youth development issues. The War also brought about changes for the OTC, but these were relatively small compared in comparison. In 1939, commissioning from the ranks was introduced so this required a change in OTC titles. Now there would be a Senior Training Corps (STC) and a Junior Training Corps (JTC). Around this time they lost the privilege of direct commissions for Certificate A holders. These name changes held throughout the War, changing again in 1948 when it was decided that the STC should become part of the Territorial Army and the JTC would form the basis of what is now the Combined Cadet Force.

By 1942, the term Army Cadet Force or ACF was again increasingly being used when discussing non school-based army cadet units, as it had become somewhat confusing to have officer cadets, school cadets and OTC cadets.

The term Army Cadet Force had originally been used way back in 1914 and yet had not been universally adopted again until 1942. One reason for this deliberate avoidance of using the term ACF was that towards the end of World War One and after there was an inevitable backlash against the government and all things military because of the appalling loss of life. It was assumed by many that the ACF was a recruiting tool for the regular army and nothing more. The word 'force' was dropped, as it sounded too militaristic and aggressive. The term used after the Great War and prior to 1942 was usually Army Cadets.

By 1942 the Army Cadet Force's numbers had risen to an impressive 180,000 all ranks. For the first time, uniform was provided free of charge and there were even grants available for the formation of new units. Staffing, however, still remained a problem. One of the most remarkable feats performed by the

Cadets practise camouflage and concealment during a training lesson.

Cadets were often taught by local Home Guard units, as this was the most reliable way of gaining knowledge and training. Some home-made armaments, IEDs and an improvised missile launcher, the efficacy of which, thankfully, would never be tested on home soil.

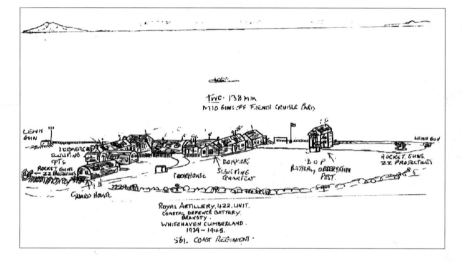

During the Second World War a cadet made this drawing of his local coastal gun battery.

Army Cadet Force during the War was sending some 100,000 cadets away to attend a week's camp during the summer of 1942. Staffing was made up of ACF, regular and reserve forces. In those days cadets were transported by train, and not coaches and minibuses as today. Consider for a moment just what a feat that was: to commandeer enough trains to move 100,000 youths in the middle of the War – it is a triumph of persuasion and bureaucratic, logistical competence bordering on genius.

All this effort paid off in terms of manpower supply, as almost 40,000 cadets per year were joining either the regular army or the Home Guard, making it a very productive exercise. Towards the end of the War, many cadet detachments were affiliated with local Home Guard units, as they had both staff and accommodation. From a training point of view, this was clearly a win-win situation, as the cadets undertook regular military tuition, while the Home Guard gained potential new members. The accepted practice was for boys of seventeen and above to serve in their local Home Guard units as active volunteers, while boys of sixteen, while not being deemed active volunteers, could provide support in some capacity; such as delivering messages or cleaning vehicles and weapons.

Canadian
cadets practise
camouflage and
concealment
training.

The value of these affiliations should not be underestimated from a social point of view. Many of the cadets had members of their own family away fighting, so at times would have looked to their Home Guard elders as something of a surrogate family. Indeed, for a few, they were their only family.

There was a particular group of individuals who took more than a passing interest in the cadets serving alongside the Home Guard units. These were the members of Churchill's secret army, the Auxiliary units. Nobody outside a chosen few had ever heard of such an organisation, as their job in the event of invasion was to act as a guerrilla force.

It was never their intention to use cadets in any combat role as such, or indeed use them in any way that would endanger their lives. It was simply the case that children can sometimes gain intelligence and information without arousing suspicion from adults. Home Guard units during training exercises would send cadets out to gain information on the whereabouts and strengths of the opposition. Typically, they would identify ranks observed, types of weapons carried and dispositions of sentries. For the cadets it was just a game. For their adult instructors, it was a simple yet extremely effective way of gathering intelligence; and in the event of invasion, it could have become a very serious game indeed.

In 1944, cadets up and down the country also found themselves playing a part in the D-Day landings. Not on the beaches of Normandy itself of course, but in massive vehicle parks that had been set up to store all the weird and wonderful craft that had been imported from the United States for the invasion. The cadets performed a myriad of jobs, ranging from painting the vehicles to loading equipment. Their labours released valuable manpower for other vital roles.

LET'S
CATCH HIM
WITH HIS
"PANZERS"
DOWN!
WE *WILL*– IF WE
KEEP 'EM FIRING!

German invasion barges at Wilhelmshaven.

Having a dig at Hitler during the Second World War was a pretty routine practice within both the Home Guard and the ACF.

Saron Robbo, D Coy 7th Cadet Battalion, Middlesex Regiment

Prior to D-Day a vehicle reserve depot was situated at the base of the King George V1 reservoir stretching from Ashford to Laleham and contained hundreds of military vehicles of all types. This was the place that as young army cadets we spent weekends during the spring and summer of 1944, we had been asked to volunteer to help prepare the vehicles before they were sent off to France.

Clad in overalls, as fifteen-year-olds we did a variety of jobs from washing off protective grease (the least favourite job) to kitting out the DKWS, the famous DUCKS (the most popular because on completion the vehicle was taken to the Thames at Laleham for a water test).

One of the jobs involved being equipped with a template and spray gun and spraying the aircraft recognition white star on the bonnets of the vehicles. To this day whenever I see pictures of the Normandy landings I wonder did I spray the star on that vehicle. For that summer we really were weekend soldiers.

One other role was performed all along the south-east coast of England in 1944-45: assisting the anti-aircraft gunners in spotting the V-1 flying bombs that were being targeted at London and other cities. Known as 'Doodle-bugs', these were Hitler's *Vergeltungswaffe*, 'vengeance weapon' and effectively his last desperate means of attacking on the home front, as he now no longer had the means of mounting an invasion.

These weapons were simple, yet effective. They were the world's first cruise missiles. They were catapulted from a ramp in either Holland or France along a set course which could not be altered. Those far below quickly realised that as long as you heard the engine you were safe, but as soon as it cut out you were in trouble as the bomb would then glide to earth.

Epsom Home Guard performing rifle drill.

Cadets were fascinated by these deadly science fiction machines, and took great pleasure in identifying them as far out from the coast as possible – enabling the gunners to engage them far more effectively than they had been able to in the early days of their operation. At the start of the War, AA gunners hit perhaps 3% of enemy aircraft. By the end of the War this figure had risen to a staggering 60%.

Gunners played tricks on the gullible cadets, telling them that the V-1s contained tiny German midget pilots, and that their job was to go out over the marshes and fields to find them. Heaven help any person of small stature who happened to bump into them while they were out and about on this deployment.

The cadet experience of the Second World War has never been matched, nor will be, as these were truly exceptional times. One legacy that survives to this day is the Army Cadet Force Association (ACFA). This was formed in 1945 and took over the role of the BNCA. Although essentially the same association as before, a name change was required as during the War both the Sea Cadet Corps and the Air Training Corps had been formed, rendering the name BNCA inappropriate.

ACF Platoon No 3 E Company 3rd Cadet Battalion, Surrey.

Coastal defence batteries were very popular with cadets as there was plenty of work for them to do within and around them.

Cadets often ambushed Home Guard vehicles as part of routine training exercises.

Princess Margaret presenting former Hurstpierpoint CCF cadet Nick Barton with the sword of honour at Sandhurst in 2001. During World War II it was suggested that the Princesses Margaret and Elizabeth would be evacuated to Canada; to which their mother famously replied, 'The children won't go without me. I won't leave without the King. And the King will never leave.' Princess Elizabeth served in uniform during the War as a member of the ATS, the Women's Auxiliary Territorial Service.

Memories of the ACF in Wartime: Oral testimony Collated by Frank Mee for the BBC Sound Archives

'In 1942, after seeing my scout hall burnt down after being bombed, I decided to join the local company of the Lincolnshire Army Cadet Force, to prepare me for any future need if the war continued, so I walked across town (everyone walked in those days), to where I had heard an ACF unit was based in an old school.

There I met a group of lads who were also interested, and I joined in, not really knowing what to expect, but I liked what we did, so, after a couple of attendances, we received our uniforms, which consisted of a battledress blouse, trousers (too long for me), a big, wide web belt, 1914 pattern, a pair of gaiters and a forage cap. This cap was to be worn on the right side of your head, with two buttons over the right eye. It took some practice to keep the hat on, particularly when you turned, as the hat spun off your head, to the anger of the NCO giving the orders! We were not issued with boots. No youth sizes, and boots were needed for the "real army". I found all the subjects interesting, including drill, weapon training and map reading, so I attended regularly every Tuesday and Thursday evening.

After a while, we moved to a Drill Hall in Augusta Street, Grimsby, which I found exciting, as there was a company of Pioneer Corps and the Home Guard based there. I used to watch the men of the Pioneer Corps doing their training, including the unlucky men on punishment drill ("Jankers"), which taught me a lot. Due to my interest in all activities, I was quickly promoted to Lance Corporal and shortly after I received a second stripe, much to the pleasure of my parents.

Because youth drum and bugle bands were a boost to the population, we formed a band and practised in a requisitioned private house in a well-to-do area and I became a side drummer. We were taught by a Canadian Air Force officer to do all the different beats and we became very proficient. There must have been some awful noise coming out of that house and I think, now, "what did the neighbours make of it?" Our dress was smartly pressed battledress, with white belts (we had the more up-to-date belts then) and gaiters. Our hair was cut to the satisfaction of the Drum Major, George Robinson, a very smart chap with his wide, coloured sash, who presented an immaculate figure.

Whether on a church parade, attendance at the Lord Mayor's Sunday, November 11th parade at the Cenotaph, displays at Grimsby Town Football Club ground (in aid of a War fund), we were, we thought, the best band amongst the youth cadet forces.

One thing we did, which I don't think the youth of today can do, was to finish band practice at about 8.30pm, walk all the way to a large dance hall (The Gaiety), where we got in at half price as we were in uniform, and get home at about 11.30pm, quite safely. We had no worries of muggings as seem rife these days. The only risk was the air raids, which were frequent.

A German tank being loaded as part of the preparations for the invasion of England.

I remember an incident when we were marching into the People's Park, in Grimsby. The Drum Major, George Robinson, threw the mace high into the air as we entered and the mace struck two telephone lines and swung like a pendulum. Well, George had to mark time, waiting for it to fall, whilst we, the band, kept on marching past him. Eventually, the mace fell and George caught up with us and all was well, but it caused a laugh with the spectators!

One evening, the regular army physical education instructor collared me and said, "we need a middleweight boxer for the team and you are it." "No, no," I replied, but after my pal Jim Fuller encouraged me, I said I would give it a go. So, yet another evening to fill my spare time. I was a busy lad!

Jogging through the darkened streets, strenuous exercises, lots of sparring (with bigger and faster boxers), kept us working hard. So it was Tuesday, Thursday drill and weapon training, Wednesdays band practice, then boxing whenever. I did enjoy it, though, and a big bonus was when we went to other cadet units or service camps in military vehicles and had good food at the various cookhouses, food that we could not get because of the rationing.

The National ACF Boxing Championships were to be held sometimes and we trained hard to enter the various county heats, so that we could be at the finals. Some of us were successful in reaching the finals, to be held later at the Royal Albert Hall.

In, I think, 1945, there was a big cadet weekend in London, with a parade of units, including many bands and the salute to be taken by HRH The Princess Margaret. Our band did not take part, but we marched in the parade. By this time, I was a Warrant Officer.

The championships? Oh, yes.

In the heat for the finals, a full programme of boxing was staged at the Drill Hall, with a paying audience. Passing a group of Yorkshire cadets, they called

out, "hey, you won't feel a thing when he hits you," and they laughed. He was a big lad and during the first two rounds he smacked me often and both rounds were judged even. My father was in the audience, so I did not want to lose, so in the third round, and after a big "rocket" from my PE instructor, I went in hard and knocked him out, much to my relief. Royal Albert Hall, here we come! But no! Although I had qualified for the finals by beating the Yorkshire cadet, we received a letter stating that on the actual date of the championships, I would be one month over the age limit, so I was eliminated. Yes, I cried with disappointment. The irony is, the cadet I knocked out in the semi final won the championships! Of course I congratulated him, although with mixed feelings.

What an experience for a young lad in wartime! During this period I was an apprentice marine fitter, doing fire watching, messenger for the Fire Service and Home Guard and had a very enjoyable, character building few years in the Lincolnshire Army Cadet Force.

Although I tried to join the regular army several times, I was either told, "Come back when you are older," or that I was in a reserved occupation as an apprentice marine fitter, so I was pleased when I was accepted and my final parade, as a Company Sergeant Major, was on 15 April 1946 and I reported to 90 Primary Training Centre, Retford, two days later, to start my 25 years (and 75 days) service in the Royal Engineers. The whole unit was on

British Prime Minister Clement Atlee (left) was a former ACF Detachment Commander and had very fond memories of his time with the cadets.

parade and I was presented with a wallet, which I had for years, but it was lost during the terrorist emergencies in the Suez Canal Zone around 1953/4. But that is another story!

My service with the ACF taught me many things which were of immense help in my military career, enabling me to complete my service as a Warrant Officer, Class One, Royal Engineers and I fully recommend any young person, boy or girl, to consider joining such an organisation as The Army Cadet Force.'

'At thirteen I lied about my age and joined the Army Cadets, you were supposed to be thirteen and a half. Issued with uniform and army boots I walked home feeling that at last I was getting nearer to being useful in the war effort. I was still at school and would be for another three years, whereas a lot of my friends had left school just before their thirteenth birthdays to go to war work.

My mother, a tailoress, took my uniform to bits then cut it to fit so when I went on Parade in the uniform for the first time I was not tied up in a sack, as most were. "A" Company Durham Light Infantry Cadets were part of the 8th Battalion covering our area, each company meeting in each of the towns around. Every company was fully manned with a waiting list to get in, I was lucky in that a large group had come of age to join the regular army, leaving positions for us new boys.

"A" Company, run by Major Downs, my best friend's father, also had the drum and bugle band, again fully manned and so keen they spent most of their time in practice sessions. One Sunday in the month was church parade, we would all assemble at the William Newton School. There was a large parade ground where we were got into order by the sergeants and our sergeant major. The officers would take posts, the band strike up and off we went out on to the road and to the church swinging along with the swagger that was drummed into us with hours of marching practice. People going to the morning service (just about everyone) would watch us march by and the local girls giggle as whispered comments came from the ranks (if you got caught doing it you lived to regret it). After the service we would march down the high street, turn and march up to our base. As we came out the girls who had followed us would be waiting at the school gates but it was the Peacocks in the band with their fancy lanyards and instruments they were all interested in.

The joy to us was we got hold of real guns, we had rifles and Bren guns to practise with, the rifles were Canadian Ross rifles, the bolt came straight back and if you did not lock it down properly; you could lose an ear as it flew backwards off the rifle. Those were soon replaced by the trusty Lee Enfield Mark Two, a First World War rifle that I loved.

I was a good shot, having being trained by Uncle Arthur on the farm since I was knee high to a rabbit. We got to shoot often in the 30 yards range at the Norton Drill Hall; 22 rifles mainly but quite a few Mark Two Lee Enfields with a lined barrel. I got into the shooting team, which meant we got quite a lot of ammunition to fire off.

Being a big lad I also got to be the Bren gunner for my section; the down side being you had to carry the thing everywhere when on training, the upside, I got to fire it a lot.

We had manoeuvres with the Home Guard and regular troops from the drill hall so got to play with mortars and heavy machine guns, it was a boy's dreamland. We also learned to dig. We marched for miles at what was called the DLI trot, march so far then run so far with our rifles at the trail. When you arrived you dug; and the funny part of it was we still enjoyed it all.

Socially we had meeting nights, games afternoons and once a month a Company Dance. By dint of having danced since I was eleven years old and knew every dance there was, I got to be MC (master of ceremonies). Having to announce each dance as the three-man band decided what we would do next, my gambit was "Right, Mary/Joan/June or whoever was in favour, you are having the next dance with me and it will be the Quickstep or Chrysanthemum waltz," whichever, and I would be first on the floor. My confidence must have been astronomical, I do not remember any refusals.

We had annual camps with the whole Battalion in military areas where we saw the latest weapons, did our mock attacks under the eyes of soldiers who had been there and were now training new men to go. It all imbued me with a longing to be older so I could get into the real War, after all a few bombs and sleeping in shelters a lot of nights was not real war, it was just a nuisance. Young, keen and daft as my dad used to say.

The training of the army cadets was quite hectic, some of our officers were from the First World War period and knew training was everything when it came to real war. We had to react instantly or be dead as they very often told us. When they thought we had assimilated enough of the training we were entered for the test called Certificate "A" part one and part two, you could not take both parts together as a lot more training was needed.

The big weekend approached for me. It was always over two days. Regular Army officers, NCOs and PT Instructors arrived from Brancepeth, the DLI depot and set to work on us boys and they did not pull any punches, if you were rubbish you got told as only an Army NCO can say it.

First the PTIs took us for the 100 yard sprint, standing long jump, running high jump and the running vault. We then went on a one-mile run followed by a one-hour march or walk, all against the clock. To finish up we did rope climb (15 feet), abdominal exercises and heaving. Before we went in for the part one test we had to be proficient in swimming, getting that test out of the way first.

After a night on the drill hall floor with two blankets and kit for a pillow, on Sunday it was close order drill, each of us taking the squad in turn, weapon training, stripping, cleaning etc, a timed map reading exercise; and then came the big one. We did fieldcraft including digging in, camouflage, then

Cadet Journal foreword by Clement Attlee.

THE CADET JOURNAL

OFFICIAL ORGAN OF THE ARMY CADET FORCE
AND OF
THE BRITISH NATIONAL CADET ASSOCIATION (INC.)
PATRON - H.M. THE KING

VOLUME VI   APRIL., 1944   No. 2

11, Downing Street,
Whitehall, S.W.

F O R E W O R D

by

The Rt. Hon. C.R. Attlee, M.P.
(Deputy Prime Minister and
Lord President of the Council).

Nearly forty years ago I was commissioned in the 1st Cadet Bn, The Queen's Regiment. I have many happy memories of those days. Now and then I meet the men who served as boys under me. Like them I learnt many valuable lessons which stood me in good stead in the war of 1914 - 18.

It is, therefore, a pleasure to me to send a message to the cadets of today in the midst of the greatest war in history. I am certain that you are learning self discipline and leadership which will help you to serve the country in war and peace.

Good wishes to you all.

C. R. Attlee

35

Section and Platoon attacks carrying out a full movement and fire manoeuvre to take an enemy position. The enemy were usually some of our big lads who already had the Cert "A" so were keen to see us lose, all good painful fun as mum said as she dressed my wounds and bruises. If King Kong had stood in my way he would have met his match, determination was all, I wanted that pass and got it. The pass rate was around 50% and having got my part one I became a Corporal.

We did annual camp at Troon in Scotland once, that was excitement, special train there and back, plus it was a nice place with plenty of dance halls. We did Catterick with the Tank Corps and Richmond with the KOYLI plus several firing range weekend camps at Whitburn. The first thing we did there was fill our palliasse (mattress) with straw, not too much (lumpy) not to little (hard). We would spend two days shooting off everything in the armoury including Vickers machine guns but only when the fishing boats got out of the way. They sometimes got a short burst around the stern if they were laggardly leaving the area when the red flag went up.

Once we had more hard training under our belts we took the Certificate "A" part two, the big one. We went off to Darlington. We slept in the Co-op Dance hall on a sprung dance floor, not the best bed in the world. Come the Saturday morning we had to start all the physical training tests once more but in reduced times. By tea time Saturday none of us felt like a night on the tiles, we were dead beat, so most were in the sack and asleep soon after tea.

It was late in the War and we had not had any raids for a long while; suddenly the siren went. We woke up hardly believing what we were hearing, but the officers said everyone up and go down the street to the shelter. We went down the stairs into the street just as two planes came in low firing their machine guns, that livened us all up, we could hear bullets ricocheting from walls and roofs. When a couple hit the street near me and went pinging away I dived into a doorway curled up like a ball and did not move until it was all clear. That must have been the very last German plane to come to our area and it very nearly got a cadet unit to paint on the cockpit. Luckily no one was hurt, we may have needed laundry for several pairs of trousers but otherwise were OK.

Next day we went to Catterick training grounds for the weapons drill, map reading and fieldcraft. When our Platoon were doing the fieldcraft we all had to take over the lead and take action as various ambushes were sprung on us. A new officer just joined from another company was leading us when we were fired on, us old boys were gone in a flash, we could hear the trigger pulled and move before the bullet left the gun. We would be flat down behind anything that would hide us in a nanosecond and I found a blade of grass can become like a brick wall to get behind.

The poor officer was left standing there in a panic looking around for a solution that was not about to show itself, like us. I don't think he knew where we had gone. Suddenly a stentorian voice shouted "Well do something, even if it is just fall down dead!" We of course were rolling about laughing. When it came to my turn I made a plan for every foot of the road we passed over until they struck with a burst of fire. I had seen the movement and given my orders, weighing up it was just a small section and we were a platoon. That gave us three to one if we did it right. It all happened so quickly, fire, outflanking movement, covering fire, charge; go through, take up firing position away from the position we had just taken because the enemy always zero their own position and drop mortars in to it. The permanent staff asked if I would do it again as they nearly missed it. That meant I had passed OK.

Lieutenant John Grayburn, VC winner and former member of the ACF, 1st (London) Cadet Force The Queen's Royal Regiment. He defended the infamous bridge at Arrnhem under constant enemy attack for three days and was eventually killed there. He is one of many cadets who have distinguished themselves in battle – the list of ACF and CCF medal recipients is long.

THE CADET JOURNAL

A FORMER MEMBER OF THE ARMY CADET FORCE WINS THE VICTORIA CROSS—SEE WITHI

**OFFICIAL ORGAN OF THE ARMY CADET FORCE
AND OF THE BRITISH NATIONAL CADET ASSOCIATION (INC)**

February, 1945   Edited by Harold Wheeler   Price 6ᵈ

At the end of the day we got presented with our full certificates and the officer in charge said we could all put on it that we had passed under enemy fire, reminding us of the night before. That event must have sharpened us all up as we got a 75% pass rate.

I was now a trained Cadet and could train others in all the infantry skills. We also got a badge for our arms that gave us even more edge with the girls, life was wonderful. As Mum sewed on my new flash Dad was heard to comment, "Young, keen, daft and now cannon fodder," but I think he was proud of me.'

III

POST WAR BLUES

As you can imagine, the end of World War II brought about yet more change for the ACF, which was no real surprise. There was now no need for a huge army or for that matter a Home Guard. Thousands of units were either disbanded or mothballed. This of course had an impact on the cadets themselves, because if they had no affiliated unit to sponsor or support them, there was no cadet unit either, as they were in many cases sharing the same staff and facilities. Cadet numbers plummeted yet again, just as they had done after the end of the First World War.

There were also new accelerants for this demise. Youth had a new-found freedom that expressed itself through music and dance. In the fifties, teenagers wanted to rock around the clock, and not march around the square. There was also the question of National Service, or conscription, which was compulsory unless you had an exceptional reason such as a medical problem or were in a reserved occupation. This system required all able-bodied young men of seventeen or over to complete eighteen months of military service. The choice of what arm of the services they served within was generally theirs, unless there was a particular shortage of manpower in a specific service. The choices were Army, Air Force, Navy, or jail.

For many young men, the idea of National Service horrified them, so the last thing that they wanted to do was enrol in the Army Cadets as they perceived it to be one and the same thing. This was of course not the case, but it did raise some issues that the ACFA had to resolve.

It is perfectly understandable why some young men would view the Army Cadet Force as nothing more than a feeder for the regular army, as its peaks and troughs in recruitment seemed to coincide with whether the country was at war or not. Picking up on this commonly held belief, the ACFA set about introducing a series of programmes and changes that would indicate a clear demarcation line between the regular and reserve forces and the cadets. For this strategy to succeed they

A happy post-war group of cadets enjoying a warm summer's day at camp.

needed to show the general public that the Army Cadet Force had a lot more to offer than was thought. So they took the organisation back almost full circle to its Octavia Hill days, it would be seen once again to have social relevance as well as military. This was extremely important, as the ACF needed to have stability and to achieve that it had to offer far more choices of activities than it had in previous decades – the teenager had arrived.

The ACFA started to modernise the ACF and make it more appealing to a broader audience. They formed a number of committees that were specifically tasked with the setting up and running of a number of sporting activities. These would eventually mature into National Championships, which survive to this day. Shooting was encouraged as a sport, rather than a military activity and included a number of competitions run at Bisley designed to encourage the development of marksmanship. A religious advisory body was set up to give the organisation spiritual guidance.

The ACFA also realised that it had to get to grips once and for all with the staffing problems that had continually dogged the ACF's development. It was accepted that it must recruit and develop its own staff, and not be so reliant on the regular and reserve forces for its manpower. Another area that needed urgent attention was training and operational guidance – to set up a unit, how to manage it and how to make it successful.

These would seem like obvious things to do, but like everything else in a big organisation, the changes took time to both ratify and implement. In March 1949 the ACFA published its first book entitled *The Official Handbook of The Army Cadet Force*. Although somewhat dry, it was in its day an extremely good book, providing sound guidance to officers as to how to run and manage a unit. Some

Cadets examine an engine as part of a skills week course.

of the advice given is as valid as ever, despite the fact that the book is now some sixty years old.

To give you some idea of the subjects covered, here are some of the chapter titles: The Historical Background, The Army and the ACF, The Cadet Officer and his Job, Training the Cadet at Home, Training the Cadet in Camp, Training the Future Citizen, The Spirit of Adventure, Games, Physical Training and Shooting, The Spiritual Side, Friends and Relations, The Product. 'The Cadet Officer and His Job' is an interesting chapter. Indeed, for any current serving ACF officer or NCO holding a Detachment Commander's role, reading it should be mandatory.

> The work of any ACF unit is a direct reflection of the devotion and abilities of its officers, and they must realize that their sole reason for being in the ACF is to train cadets to become 'good British citizens', who, when they put on battle-dress, become 'good British soldiers.'
>
> The furtherance of the aim of the ACF is a responsibility which must be recognized as such by any man who accepts work in the movement. To mark the acceptance of such responsibility, the officer is given his Majesty's commission. This is, under present circumstances, seldom actually seen, and it is worth while reproducing the wording to make clear the charge laid upon the man who is privileged to hold it.
>
> 'GEORGE THE SIXTH, by the Grace of God of Great Britain, Northern Ireland, and the British Dominions beyond the Seas, King, Defender of the Faith, etc.
>
> 'To our Trusty and Well Beloved ......

Canadian cadets preparing for a large field exercise.

Greetings! We, reposing especial Trust and Confidence in your Loyalty, Courage and Good Conduct, do by these Presents Constitute and Appoint you to be an officer in our Territorial Army from the...day of......19... You are therefore carefully and diligently to discharge your duty as such in the Rank of ...... or in such other Rank as We may from time to time hereafter be pleased to promote or appoint you to, of which a notification will be made in the London Gazette, or in such other manner as may for the time being be prescribed by Us in Council, and you are in such manner and on such occasions as may be described by Us to exercise and well discipline in arms both the inferior officers and men serving under you and use your best endeavours to keep them in good order and discipline. And We do hereby Command them to Obey you as their superior Officer and you to observe and follow such Orders and Directions as from time to time you shall receive from us, or any your superior Officer , according to the Rules and Discipline of War, in pursuance of the Trust reposed in you.'

'To our Trusty and Well Beloved.' This is a magnificent start, a source of inspiration and encouragement. In this matter His Majesty is acting as Head of the Nation. It is not the Sovereign alone, but, in the Churchillian phrase, the broad masses of our peoples that place trust and confidence in Cadet officers to play their part in the training and education of the next generation.

Not a drop left, observes a young cadet in a sand-bagged position.

… Each individual has his own particular virtues and talents, and he should serve in a post where these assets can be used to the best advantage. The company commander and his immediate staff are in direct contact with the cadets. Behind them the whole organization of battalion, county supply and specialist officers exists, not to add complications, but to service the companies.

All must be complementary each to each. Rank indicates a differentiation of function, and an added responsibility in a wider field, but does not necessarily indicate importance to the ACF. A young platoon commander leading twenty boys may be doing valuable work which will bear immediate results in boys' lives. There is nothing more important than that.

Hurstpierpoint cadets proudly show off an award after winning a shooting competition.

One might well compare the organization of the ACF with a football team. The sub-unit commanders are playing at forward. Battalion is at half-back, and HQ in goal. We may hope that HQ will not see too much of the ball, and the better the game goes, the greater fun it is for the forwards …

There is a very great difference between the work of the ACF officer and the Army officer. The great majority of ACF officers are recruited from men who have had Army experience, but valuable as that experience is, it is not by any means a sufficient qualification for work with boys, unless the essential differences are comprehended and accepted. It will be readily seen that there are two main factors that constitute the difference – the age of the cadets, and the voluntary nature of their work …

The cadet is not yet adult. In many cases he may like to think he is, and he will be encouraged to develop the attributes of manhood, but he should not be treated as though he were capable of full adult activities, either mental or physical.

The cadet age is one of adventure and enjoyment. Training must, and can be, not merely interesting, but real fun. Work and play can be so intermingled that it is difficult to tell just where one begins and the other ends. There can be as much real enjoyment in map reading as in a game of soccer …

The cadet Movement is a voluntary one and we may hope that it always will be. The idea of voluntary service forms part of the great heritage of the British nation, and it is one that must be cherished and guarded … Officers and cadets who join the ACF are expected, while members of the Force, to fulfil those duties which fall to their lot. A responsibility voluntarily assumed is no less – indeed, is often more – binding than one imposed by other circumstances.

Enter when you like; leave when you like; but when in, play to the rules, and keep your word. … It has been shown that one of the two main differences between the Army and the Cadet Force lies in this question of voluntary leadership. In the Army the officer can give an order and must be obeyed. Behind the officer is a long and imposing list of sanctions, all carefully detailed in King's Regulations. In the Cadet Force there are no such sanctions. …

Discipline and morale in a voluntary movement can be as high, and often higher, than that in formations governed by the element of compulsion.

Cadets escort a convoy of old Bedford trucks to a local community event.

Another generation of cadets happy after winning a shooting competition.

There is no higher form of obedience than that obtained by the willing subjection of the will of one individual to that of another for the good of the whole. Such discipline is rooted in one thing and one alone – Respect. The cadet may respect his unit, his uniform, or the Force as a whole, but the immediate cause of his loyalty and interest will be respect for his officer …

The voluntary nature of cadet service has many very valuable advantages. The boys are keen, at any rate when they join. The preservation of that keenness is the leader's task. Given keenness and enthusiasm, all things are possible. Once cadets have been shown the reasons -and this is essential – they will work cheerfully and well under good leadership.

Drill parades become a matter of pride, personal appearance smartens, and the many and varied activities detailed in this book are tackled with zest. Success with cadets demands two things. There must be personal leadership by the officer, and the cadets themselves must feel that they have a real stake in the unit. The former can be achieved by personal example and individual interest, so that the cadets do realize that their officer is not only a figure on parade, but one who is interested in them as persons …

To some readers there may appear to be a difficulty in the officer/cadet relationship. There need be no such difficulty, or, if there is it will be found to exist in the mind of the officer rather than that of the boy. When on parade, every effort should be made to make that parade as smart and formal as possible. Boys like a good show. They have no tolerance for the sloppy or the second best. On parade, the officer is the commander and should expect and require all the usual outward signs of respect due to his rank. Off parade, he can become rather the elder brother. (This expression is used in no sentimental sense.) He must be ready to share their interests and assist their projects. In ACF matters, he will give a lead; in others, he will be prepared to help the boy's own ideas. There is no contradiction here. The cadets will accept this. They see nothing incongruous in being drilled on company parade one evening by a man whose advice they ask on their hobbies the next …

There should be no attempt at imitation sanctions, which are, indeed forbidden. Such things as imitation company office, or punishments manufactured within the unit, are quite useless and have no basis in actuality, and should therefore be avoided; while the institution of 'punishment fatigues', either in headquarters or in camp, are not only valueless immediately but in the long run have the effect of debasing work which should be an accepted part of the unit's life. Indeed, the very word 'fatigue' is best avoided. In a well-run unit the chores will be accepted as part of the duties which fall to all in turn, and accepted cheerfully. This spirit is killed as soon as some necessary chore is used as a punishment medium.

The one complete and ultimate sanction is the expulsion of a cadet from his unit. For a first, and sometimes second, serious offence, the proper punishment is to suspend the cadet for two, three or four weeks. This works very much better than might be expected. The drill is simple. The errant cadet is told that he must not come near the unit for so long, and that at the end of that time he may apply for reinstatement.

It might be assumed that no boy thus caused to lose face would come back, but that is not so. Usually the combination of a guilty conscience and adverse public opinion will produce the necessary degree of repentance, and back he comes …

Finally, as we have said, there is expulsion. This will only be used on the rarest occasions. The expulsion of a boy is generally, thought not always, an admission of failure by the officer concerned. This fact must be fairly faced …

Often a visitor to a unit, when numbers are small, will be greeted by the remark, 'Oh, we have just had a clear out of 'dead wood.' It is good to clear 'dead wood,' but why did it die? The good officer will never rest until he knows the answer. The knowledge will enable him to save other wood from becoming dead in future. Added to the respect for the officer there is also the respect for tradition, and this has a very strong bearing on discipline. Founded on the pride of the Regiment, tradition can also be guided until it is the pride of the unit, and the force of tradition, specially when in the hands of cadet NCOs, can be a potent factor in the preservation of morale. …

The ACF officer has to blend the requirements of military and citizenship training. His methods must be to use the military structure and mould his

A study in youthful concentration. 'I think it goes in here Sir.' Was this you?

other activities around the central frame. This requires the development of a special technique, or cadet method. The cadet method, as advocated in this handbook, is something peculiar to the pre-service organizations. The ACF is a youth movement in its own right. Its methods are peculiarly its own, not a pale shadow of others. Nonetheless, much may be learnt from study of other youth work. For well over fifty years there has been established a fund of experience, largely the result of work by early pioneers in many branches of youth work …

… The task of the officer is to give the cadets not only what they want, but what they need. There is usually a vast difference between the two. First, the boy must be given what he wants (within reason). Why did he join at all? The platoon officer will find this fact out early. Perhaps he was attracted by uniform, by the sport, by the fact that friends were in the unit, or his father in the regiment.

Whatever it was that attracted him, the bill must be met. The officer will seek to ensure that whatever attracted in the shop window is, in fact, on sale in the shop. Then, by using the boy's initial desires, he will lead the individual on to those interests, activities and training which will develop the weak spots of his character and discourage any unsatisfactory traits.

Much, if not all, will depend on the personal attributes of the officer. He must be prepared to use all resources of his own or his colleagues to achieve the desired result. The task will be done by first earning the boy's respect, next by gaining his confidence, and then by leading him into the ways of a soldier and a gentleman.

As important and successful as the introduction of the *Army Cadet Force Handbook* was, more effort and direction was still needed if the ACF was to go mainstream. It was also around this time that the ACF took to hosting regular conferences and study groups as a means of fostering new ideas and developing a common 'Best Practice' strategy. But there still remained the question of time lag and standards implementation, as not every battalion or county got with the programme at the same time or to the same level of competence.

In 1955 this situation was rectified when the King George VI Memorial Trust Fund donated money to the ACFA to help it fund further training courses. Their grant was immediately used to fund a series of eight-day courses in each of the command areas. They proved to be an instant hit with just about everyone in the ACF. These courses helped to standardise training across the ACF, before their introduction matters relating to staff education had been very ad hoc.

In 1957 the Amery Committee was set up with the purpose of reviewing the ACF and giving it direction for the future. Its recommendations were extremely positive, resulting in a number of significant changes. The ACF would now be more streamlined in its set-up, and better positioned to respond to change. It would also shed outdated training and operational practices. The original course set up with the grant from The King George VI Memorial Trust would now be permanent under the name KGVI. A Cadet Training Centre was to be established at Frimley Park for this course and others.

There were numerous other changes and additions during this period, one of the most important being the introduction of the Duke of Edinburgh's Award Scheme (D of E) in 1956. The scheme set down a series of challenges and activities both mental and physical, all designed to test the young in a beneficial and positive way.

The ACF was one of the first youth organisations to embrace the Duke of Edinburgh's Award Scheme, serving as a 'test bed' during its pilot stages and then ultimately as an operating authority of the Scheme. For the ACF, the D of E scheme fitted perfectly into its long-term plans to develop both adventure training and citizenship. Almost all of the scheme's requirements were already to be found within the comprehensive syllabus of the ACF but what was needed was a focus and greater public recognition. The scheme provided a tangible symbol of achievement with respect to citizenship and character development, aims emphasised in the new Charter formulated by the Amery Report. By the end of the fifties, the ACF had modernised itself in a way that many would have thought impossible ten years before; which was just as well, as it was about to face a completely new set of challenges.

IV

THE TIMES THEY ARE A CHANGIN'

The changes brought about by the Amery Report would be nothing compared to what was about to come following the 1960 Albemarle Report, a comprehensive analysis of 'youth culture'. The Albemarle Report was a far more comprehensive look at every aspect of youth development and affected all youth organisations and schools. It was a watershed in the history of youth work, and marked the beginning of the expansion and professionalisation of youth work in the 1960s and 1970s. The reason for its commissioning was the conception by authority of a youth crisis brought about by a growing population whose values were changing and morals had apparently plummeted. In the simplest sense, society was becoming frightened of its own children.

This coincided with the end of National Service, which led to inevitable demands that it should be brought back. To blame every problem on the ending of this temporary conscription measure was naive as there were plenty of other factors. For one thing, some young men deeply resented their freedom being taken away and reacted in a rebellious manner once their service tenure ended.

Young men were not just teenagers in the sixties and seventies – they were members of cultural and musical tribes, the Mods and Rockers, Beatniks, Hippies – and if you did not belong to any of them, you were a Square! For the Army Cadet Force, reaching out to these young people was seen as a fair challenge – as by this time in its history, it certainly had enough knowledge and experience to try. This confidence was in part justified as the ACF had just celebrated its centenary and was viewed by the Albemarle Report as being something of a beacon organisation. That is not to say that it could not improve, as there were still issues yet to be resolved, such as making the organisation more inclusive and accountable in its training practices. The key attribute in favour of the ACF was the fact that it was a voluntary organisation and not mandatory, which was largely the case with the CCF. If a young teenage boy joined the ACF he was exercising his freedom of

Cadets from the seventies, some with the hairstyles you might expect.

Cadets from West London pose for a unit photo.

choice, and would therefore be far more likely to accept an adult instructor who was also a volunteer. This echoes an old ACF saying: 'You don't have to put up with me, but equally I don't have to put up with you.' The Albemarle Report saw that it was absolutely vital to engage young people and not attempt to dominate them. It was important for teenagers to see that there were adults who watched their back and had their best interests at heart.

The ACF leaders were masters at working with young boys once they had enrolled, but how do you get teenagers to join up when they are more interested in where the latest hot band is playing? It was of course new territory for the ACF as they had never had to compete against so many other choices.

The answer to the dilemma was to let the teenagers be cadets during their time at their detachments, and be ravers if they so wished during their free time: in essence, give them their freedom of choice, as long as they perform their duties competently, diligently and respectfully while on duty.

As we have seen, until the end of the Second World War the ACF's recruitment was a series of peaks and troughs, dependent on whether we were at war or not. In the fifties, sixties and seventies, despite the fact that we had the Korean War, The Malaya and Borneo conflicts, The Troubles in Northern Ireland, as well as a host of other mini wars, the ACF's recruitment had remained constant, with only the odd blip now and again. This relative stability was all down to the hard work of the ACFA who tirelessly publicised the unappreciated yet valuable citizenship aspect of the organisation to all, thereby dispensing with the myth that the ACF was just a junior branch of the regular army and nothing more.

What was it like to be a cadet in the ACF during this period? This account by one of my Cadet Force colleagues sheds some light.

Clive Clahar

I joined the Army Cadet Force in 1966 when I was only 11, (just after England had won the World Cup) thanks to my best friend Geral Dunworth, who was then a member. Right from the word go I enjoyed what was on offer, and took part in every activity that was going. My unit was originally badged Royal Artillery when I joined up, but eventually changed to Royal Engineers, which it still is to this day.

Before our current purpose-built building was constructed, I helped to build the original wooden one when I was a cadet, as did all of my mates. In those days we wore itchy scratchy Battle dress with horrible hairy shirts, which I was glad to see the back of as they were so uncomfortable and impractical. I hated having to use the blanco and brass polish that we were required to use as it took so long to achieve any sort of effect. The only part of the uniform I really liked was the greatcoat that they issued to us, as it was something of a fashion item – especially the ATC ones, which the hippies loved.

We all looked forward to attending annual camp, as for many of us it was the only holiday we ever got to go on. We usually travelled by train

A Canadian cadet in summer kit poses with another colleague in period uniform from the previous century.

A weekend in the field. Can anyone identify these cadets? Are you one of them? The author would love to know.

Cadets trying out
a new cabaret
routine for their
forthcoming
camp.

or 3-tonner as during those times, coach travel was virtually unheard of. Another odd thing was that we even carried our Lee Enfield 303s on the trains some of the time as we went about our training, something that would never be allowed today.

In terms of training, we all worked hard towards gaining our Certificate 'A" and once passed we were senior cadets. We could then fire the Bren gun, which was great fun. We all loved music at the time, and in my case it was Jimi Hendrix that I loved to listen to as he was a musical genius.

I always look back with found memories of this period of Army Cadet Force history and feel that it was the best time to have been a cadet as there were far less restrictions on what you could or couldn't do. Basically, everything got done by common sense and not form filling.

As soon as I was old enough I became an instructor, which would have been around 1971. During my service one of my officers (now retired) was Captain Alan Hart, who originally had been my Sgt Major when I was younger. We served side by side for almost thirty years, and are still friends to this day. At the time of my becoming an instructor, we faced the possible threat of the IRA and were required to post cadets on the gates with drill weapons as some sort of deterrent. That of course would never happen now.

Canadian cadet giving a Bren gun lesson.

I even remember the issue of dark green civilian waterproof tops as a means of hiding our uniforms from possible terrorists.

By the mid-seventies, we had rid ourselves of battle dress and wore denims which were little more than overalls. These awful uniforms thankfully didn't lasted for long as we acquired British Army issue combats, which made us feel that we were really part of something very special. By the early eighties, I noticed a change in the ACF in that our numbers grew at a faster rate than I can recall over the previous years. I can only put this down to a change in teenage trends.

I have now served in the Army Cadet Force for 43 years, and have reached the dizzy heights of Sgt Major. I regard it as the best thing that I have ever done in my life. My fellow NCOs and officers often tease me about how long I have served, often joking about how my first weapon must have been a musket! I however have the last laugh, as the ACF has given me many fantastic memories that I will treasure forever.

And before anyone asks, no, He was not a drummer boy at the Battle of Waterloo.

Moving on into the Eighties, the ACF enjoyed a very short-term surge in its recruitment brought about by a patriotic reaction to the Iranian Embassy Siege in London in 1980 and the Falklands War in 1982. In the case of the Iranian Siege, the sight of black-clad, ninja-like SAS soldiers abseiling down the wall of the Embassy and storming it in a spectacular manner was just too much for any teenager to witness without drawing some sort of reaction – often a b-line straight down to the nearest army recruiting office or cadet detachment. Their favourite regiment to join? The SAS.

CCF cadets practising radio procedure.

In some areas, cadet recruitment soared by almost 200% just after the siege and then returned to normal pre-1980 levels shortly after. Then in April 1982 Argentina invaded the Falkland Islands. (The news of this invasion caused great consternation to the many who believed that the Falkland Islands were off the coast of Scotland.) Some elements of the ACF promptly volunteered their cadets and adults to local military garrisons to help them out in any capacity that would relieve soldiers for more pressing duties. This really did help our armed forces to speed up their preparations for deployment to the Falklands.

The ATC and Sea Cadet Corps also helped out, and in one particular case they stripped an old moth-balled warship of its rust and cleaned it up as best they could, as there was a possibility that it might have to be pressed back into service on account of shipping losses sustained during this short but bloody war.

At the time there were many who were extremely pleased to see our youth respond in such a positive and supportive way. As a result, the ACF enjoyed a very successful 125th Anniversary in 1985. A special commemorative post card book was produced, which illustrated the changing face of the ACF. Some of its images are reproduced here.

As the eighties drew to a close, the ACF realised that there was still more work to be done to make it a more inclusive mirror of society. A decision was taken that would have monumental significance for the ACF, and would require a seismic shift in its attitude, policy and organisation.

Prince of Wales
CCF on parade in
Kenya, 1963.

Probably one
of my favourite
photos from a
carefree world
long past,
showing cadets
being cadets.
Circa 1955.

The British Army had Clive of India; the ACF has Clive of Acton.

The hut that Sgt Major Clahar helped build. See page 90.

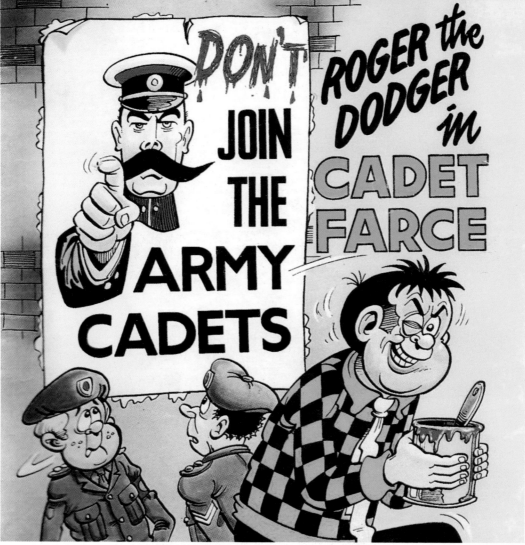

Rodger the Dodger having a go at the Army Cadet Force. (Courtesy of D C Thompson.)

Young Clive at 11, in the middle of the front rank.

A very rare image depicting cadets armed with US M16 assault rifles.

A CCF cadet
scanning his area
for signs of life.

CCF cadets
practising fire
fighting drills.

Cadets on
board an Abbot
self-propelled
gun.

Another one for
the Unit album,
courtesy of the
Royal Artillery.

ACF 125th
Anniversary
Badge.

V

FEMALES JOIN THE ACF

If you are female and you have got this far reading this book without throwing it away in frustration, thank you for you patience and understanding and my apologies for your non-appearance up to now. You know the reason, there were no girls in either the ACF or the CCF up until this point; and if some had got their way, that would have still been the case. Girls in the ACF and CCF are now a key part of both organisations and make up some 25 per cent of their respective cadet strengths. They are here to stay – so those reactionaries just had to get used to it.

There were two initial objections. Firstly of course, while the ACF had immense experience of how to nurture and educate boys, it had absolutely no knowledge of how to deal with girls. Secondly, there were mundane, practical issues, such as the installation of washroom facilities. These issues got the ACF into hot water with the press. On 26 June 1999 the *Scottish Evening News* printed an article headlined 'Girls told about turn by "Sexist" Cadet Force.' A Scottish county had been running a recruitment campaign but had been turning girls away on the grounds that they did not have the money to provide facilities for them. This was not an isolated incident, as there were numerous other cadet units in the same boat.

The MoD tried to deflect the criticism, stating that it did not have the financial resources to kit out each and every cadet detachment for females. Their defence, fortunately, fell on deaf ears. For many in the ACF at the time of this controversy, an improvise, adapt and overcome attitude prevailed, and as a result the first few females stormed the ACF/CCF male bastion. To have female cadets, however, you needed to have female adult instructors in place; but you couldn't get female instructors unless you had female cadets – Catch 22.

I remember this being a frustrating time. As the OC of a detachment I am proud to say I was one of the first to accept female cadets, and my unit was something of a pioneer in this new endeavour. I remember announcing to the boys one

A young female cadet from Rugby School CCF enjoys a conversation with her inspecting Officer.

Cadets Ria Black, Chelsea Banks and Stef Briton practise loading drills on a 25 pounder field gun.

night that we would be accepting girls, which evoked instant despondency and consternation. Encouraged by the overwhelming enthusiasm, I asked some of the older boys to start bringing down their sisters and school friends as a means of testing the water. We started our initial female training cadre with just three girls. Although heavily outnumbered by the boys, they were enthusiastic and very keen to learn, so I made every effort to include them in all the activities. But we had no female instructors, so therefore could not take girls away on training weekends until some were assigned to us.

For the boys in the unit, it was also a difficult time, as I made the decision that if the girls could not go on training weekends then neither could they – as we were one unit and not two. I had made it clear to the girls that they would not be getting any special treatment from me – it would be a case of exactly the same rules and regulations for all. Bear in mind that prior to the arrival of the girls, the unit used to be away three weekends out of four, so grounding them until a female instructor arrived was not a popular decision. The cadets however respected what I was trying to do and worked harder in other areas to take their minds off this temporary blip. It was very much a case of what we could do, rather than what we could not. Eventually our patience paid off and we got a female instructor; we were in business at last.

It was also around the time of my first female instructor's arrival that one of the girls asked if she could bring down some of her classmates. I of course said yes, but what followed was a shock. One night she arrived at the unit with 17 of her classmates and friends, and they all wanted to join up. It didn't end there either, as another eight joined up the following week.

Cadets take a running jump as part of a diversionary attack on a coastal fort.

The arrival of so many girls gave the boys a wake-up call, as the new arrivals were ambitious and wanted to compete against all the other units within our sector as soon as possible – and in all activities. Within months they were really making their mark. Nothing ever seemed to get them down. There was a noticeable difference in attitude. When a boy joins a unit he usually presents a front of 'I'm used to playing with guns so there's not much you can teach me.' With the girls, it was very much 'I know absolutely nothing about any of this – so please teach me everything you know.' Eventually, when we went on annual camps and had 'Best Cadet' competitions within the 'Star Groups', our girls swept the board in every class. This of course upset the boys and spurred them on, as they were being shown up at every level.

In due course, a healthy competitive spirit developed that got the best out of everyone, creating a very close knit group that were up for any sort of challenge. I have to say that taking on girls was the best decision that I have ever made within the ACF. My experience is of course not isolated as many other detachments up and down the country went through similar experiences and are clearly now the better for it. What follows is a personal account from one of my senior girls regarding her ACF career.

Liz Costello

In January 2004, my best friend persuaded me to go with her to the local army cadet unit in Harrow, she had heard about it from a close family friend, who was an instructor at the detachment. As a recruit I never thought I would achieve so much; five years on I have numerous awards, have visited

Female cadet on manoeuvres in Cyprus.

Cadet Sgt Major Liz Costello of 201 (Harrow) has just about seen and done it all during her time with ACF.

many different places and have experienced this with the close friends I have made. The Army Cadet Force has helped my self confidence, and has also helped me progress my leadership and teamwork skills.

When I first joined the ACF, I was shy but determined; I wanted to achieve a lot. I enjoyed learning new skills, especially fieldcraft; putting on cam cream and being able to participate in fire fights, it gave me an adrenaline rush. Physical activity is also another one of my favourite things – participating in sporting competitions and going on assault courses; I love a challenge.

On my first annual camp I won the best 1 star runner up award, which was a shock but I had worked hard through the two weeks. I also got promoted to Lance Corporal. Although I was only a Lance Corporal I was in charge of the junior section, making sure everybody got up and was ready for the events they had to participate in. This gave me more confidence in myself and made me realise how much responsibility I had as an NCO. I also took part in an expedition and did my Duke of Edinburgh, which developed my teamwork skills.

My second camp was tough. I was in charge of a billet of fifteen girls, the majority of them my age and older, making sure the billet was immaculate every morning and that they were out in time for first parade. I had not been put in this situation before, it taught me to be more confident in myself and show that I could successfully lead a team of people. At the end of camp I had won best 2 star runner up I was quite disappointed because I had worked hard but knew I could have been more serious, this gave me an incentive to work harder.

As a Corporal I participated in many events; cross country and athletics at National level where I won silver and gold medals. I did my JCIC (junior cadet

What's for breakfast then? It has proved to be impossible to establish with any certainty when the very first (and very few) females joined the ACF or the CCF. There are indications that it could have been as early as 1982 – with female instructors joining even earlier – but this has not been confirmed.

instructor course) and passed with a grade of B+ and a recommendation to SCIC. This enabled me to teach others at my detachment which gave me a big confidence boost. I went on fieldcraft weekends, learning new and exciting tactics and passed a junior first aid course; which made me realise how important it is to be able to help others when in a dangerous situation. I also had the once-in-a-lifetime experience of going to Hong Kong for two weeks; it was amazing. My third annual camp was the most enjoyable, throughout the two weeks the three stars had to work together, especially when doing map and compass! During this camp I was in charge of a section for most of the camp and was also in charge of my billet; I had to show discipline and authority. This camp I worked my hardest, during training I was serious and tried my best but still had fun during NAAFI! I was proud of myself when I won the best three star award and was promoted to Sergeant.

Not long after annual camp, I was promoted to Staff Sergeant on a group weekend, however I gave my rank in because I felt I was not prepared for this promotion, I needed to earn it. Teaching others gave me the most confidence because I had to teach both cadets and NCOs. I was told by others how hard SCIC was, so I was nervous; me and my sister were the only Sergeants on the course so the instructors would expect better from us. It was a challenge but I passed the course and won the best cadet award. I was surprised, but having to march out in front of sector was my proudest moment. When I got my promotion to Staff Sergeant I felt that I had definitely earned my rank.

After annual I went for a week of adventure training in Wales for my BTEC in public services. I went gorge walking, rock climbing and canoeing. I had a really enjoyable time although I ended up covered in bruises! I got the grade Distinction in my BTEC. I was now the highest rank in my unit, which I never thought I would be. I now had to make the big decisions; making sure everything ran smoothly. I was awarded the Deputy Lieutenant award as the outstanding cadet and member of the community and took part in the Outreach programme. This programme was gruelling; having to work with a large number of disadvantaged teenagers. It was tough but I had fun participating in the activities; pony trekking, rock climbing, hill walking, It taught the teenagers to work as a team. I did feel proud of the group I was helping to mentor when they won a competition on the last night, it showed that we had helped them to work together.

Just before my fifth annual camp I was promoted to Sergeant Major (WO2). This annual camp was different; I had to teach the 3 stars. At the end of annual I was made Group Sergeant Major. Being in charge of more than 120 cadets is a big responsibility! On my first group weekend I lost my voice due to the amount of shouting I had to do.

Throughout my time in cadets I have taken part in Remembrance Parades, paying my respects to those who have fought and died for our country; participated in fund raising events; bag packing and unit open days and have been able to help out at events for the community.

During my time at cadets I have learnt many new skills which will help me in my education and also in the future. It has taught me self discipline, enhanced my confidence and leadership skills and had also taught me the importance of teamwork. I have been on exchanges, expeditions and adventure training. I have also made many life long friends and have had many experiences that I could have never have dreamed of if I had not joined the ACF.

VI

A TRAGEDY AND ITS AFTERMATH

In 1998, the organisation faced a crisis that demanded: an entire root and branch review of its operational and training methods following the tragic death of a 15-year-old cadet, Clare Shore.

Although not the first fatality to occur in the ACF's history, the circumstances surrounding the loss of this young girl were such that the ACF could not be allowed to continue to train cadets as before. Clare lost her life after a Land Rover struck her as she was crawling through grass during a night exercise, the driver totally unaware of her presence.

There was an extensive enquiry into her death that found nobody specifically responsible. This was not acceptable to the HSE (Health and Safety Executive) who considered bringing a Crown Censure against the Ministry of Defence – which is basically the equivalent of a civil Crown Court prosecution. It was only rescinded when cast iron assurances were given that procedures would change to make both individuals and management more responsible and accountable for the planning, running and execution of ACF training.

The changes that immediately followed were indeed far reaching, and affected everyone in the ACF. To give you an example of how these changes affected us at ground level, prior to Clare Shore's death, a weekend authorisation to train document was just one page, and required the following basic information:

When are you going?
Where are you going?
Who is going ?
How long are you going for?
How many are going?
What transport, food, weapons and ammunition do you require?

Today, things are very different. Before we go anywhere outside our unit's base we need formal authorisation and a completed detailed RA (risk assessment). The more demanding the activity, the more paperwork you need to fill in. Typically this would extend to about 10 pages of information. However, in one event I organised involving the use of explosives, power boats and a field exercise, my paperwork consisted of 173 pages of RA documents, authorisation forms and parental consent forms. It took me four days to complete. This of course is an extreme example, but it does give you some idea of how much things have changed; and quite rightly. We as officers and instructors are acting *in loco parentis*, and it is our duty and that of our superiors to ensure that everything that we do is as safe as humanly possible.

Officers, Instructors and Cadets about to receive a safety briefing.

All things considered the ACF's safety record is exceptionally good compared to similar organisations. But it is still trying to do better. While admitting that we are not really comparing like with like, it is instructive to know that since 1990 the ACF has lost two cadets and two adults in accidents, and the regular army, three times its strength, has suffered 1,748 fatalities in non-combat related incidents in and around barracks. It is fair to point out that if we organise challenging and demanding activities and run them safely for our cadets, they will probably not create their own versions – which would by definition be far more dangerous.

In addition to developing risk-reducing strategies, the ACF also spends a lot of time, money and effort in training its staff to as high a standard as possible, considering the fact that our officers and instructors are volunteers and not full-time employees. In addition to all of the practical and theoretical safety training provided, all staff are required to undertake a CRB (Criminal Records Bureau) check and an SC (Security Clearance) verification before being allowed to work with cadets. All instructors follow the SST (Safe System of Training) process. There are four elements to SST: Safe Persons, Safe Equipment, Safe practice and Safe Place. In addition to this code of practice, all Cadet Force Adult Volunteers (CFAVs)

A cadet lets rip with a Bren gun while walking – not a chance of that today.

Cadets collecting live rounds! It would never be permitted.

are required to take an MST (Military Skills Test) every six months so as to ensure that their skill levels are up to standard. The test itself involves a weapons handling test, a map and compass exercise and an exam to test the instructor's ability to use the ACF's Cadet Training Safety Precautions book. Safety is paramount in the ACF, and every aspect of training, vehicle usage and weapons handling is scrutinised in depth at every possible opportunity so as to maintain the highest best practice standards. The ACF is one of the most safety-conscious youth organisations operating, with professional standards that are the envy of many.

VII

BEYOND THE SHORES

If we could go back fifty years and talk to cadets from a past era about their most treasured holiday memory, many would probably have said it was their annual camp, as that was their only holiday. The idea of an overseas cadet trip, well that would have been truly unimaginable; but today there are plenty of overseas travel and exchange opportunities on offer – and all that is required to experience them is a spirit of adventure. For those that do participate, life is never really the same afterwards.

I had the privilege of participating in the Hong Kong exchange programme in 2006, along with four other officers and adult instructors and twenty cadets. This particular exchange programme only started the year before, after a delegation from the Hong Kong Adventure Corps came over to the UK to participate in our annual camp at Otterburn.

It is a Chinese custom that if somebody treats you well, you must repay their kindness ten-fold. However, when we visited Hong Kong there must have been a mistranslation somewhere as they repaid us a thousand-fold. Every day our hosts would compete with one another to see who could give us the best day out: diving, boat trips, cultural visits, police academy visits, Kung Fu lessons and battlefield tours

The simple comment that summed up this trip came from one of cadets as he phoned his parents to let them know how he was getting along. He said 'this is the best thing that I have ever done in my life, it's been absolutely fantastic.' This has always stuck with me, and it drives me to encourage my cadets not to miss out on opportunities. I very much subscribe to the view that travel is the best education that you can get. My Sector, Middlesex & North West, is of course not alone in offering such wonderful opportunities, as each and every county and CCF unit has access to programmes.

One of the best providers of overseas travel to both the ACF and CCF is CCAT (Combined Cadet Adventure Training). These people take care of everything, from

A British Cadet tries out an American AR-15 assault rifle in Hong Kong.

organising an adventure training course in the Welsh mountains to sending cadets to Bavaria for a week's skiing. All the risk assessments, planning and organisation is taken care of by them. These courses are also heavily subsidised.

The Canada exchange programme is the oldest and best established exchange programme in both the ACF and CCF, with competition for places extremely fierce. The exchange is made up of a number of separate packages that include adventure training, mountain climbing and shooting. The exchange is very long in duration – lasting 54 days – so stamina and determination is a key requirement. And the cost of all this – a staggering £125! Believe it or not, if you turn up for the course you actually get your money back. What a deal.

Cadets have also visited Australia, Bermuda, Brunei, Cyprus, Egypt, India, Jamaica, Kenya, Malta, Morocco Nepal, Norway, Pakistan and Sweden. In the case of my own Detachment, since 2005 cadets and adults from my unit have been to Austria (twice) Bavaria (three times) Canada, Cyprus, France (twice), and Hong Kong. So we do get about.

Other Nations

As impressive as our cadet force history is, there are other army-inspired youth organisations abroad that also have a long and distinguished history. Some are school-based CCF units that are a legacy of our old colonial past, others are organisations just like the British ACF. A number of these organisations, the Australian Army Cadets, the Hong Kong Adventure Corps, the Royal Canadian Army Cadets and the various Cadet Corps and Cadet Forces of the Caribbean that make up the West Indies have very close connections to both the Army Cadet Force and the CCF.

Australian Army Cadets

The AAC is authorised under Section 62 of the Defence Act of 1903. Like the ACF, it models itself on the values and traditions of its Army, and has cadet units in every state and territory in Australia. Cadets may join the AAC at the age of 12 years and 6 months, and can remain a cadet until they are 18. In certain special cases they can remain until they are 20. Like the ACF, a cadet in the AAC is not part of the armed forces.

The aim of the AAC is to develop an interest in the Army and its traditions; to encourage cadets to continue military or community service; to give cadets a foundation of military knowledge and discipline; to develop the qualities of leadership, self-discipline, self-reliance and initiative; and to provide training that may contribute to Army common induction training.

The AAC can trace its history back to 1865, with The King's School and Newington College vying for the honour of who has the oldest Cadet Corps. However, the honour of the first official unit goes to St Mark's Collegiate School, Macquarie Fields, New South Wales, who formed in 1866. As the cadet units expanded, King Edward VII established the Commonwealth Cadet Corps in Australia on 16 July 1906. On 2 May 1970, the Duke of Edinburgh presented his banner as a gift to the Corps following his appointment as Colonel-in-Chief of the Australian Cadet Corps in 1963. The presentation took place at Victoria Barracks, Sydney.

Since its establishment, the Corps has experienced three name changes, firstly to the Australian Cadet Corps (ACC), then the Australian Army Cadet Corps, and in 2001 to the Australian Army Cadets. Cadet units are usually based on a company structure, whereas a larger unit would be based upon a battalion structure. Australia also has school-based cadet units, the equivalent of the CCF.

1911 was the year of King George V's Coronation, and although Australia was to be represented officially by both its Army and Navy, there were no plans to involve its army cadets. An Australian officer by the name of Major G W Wynne decided to invite himself and 200 cadets to the Coronation. That meant a return journey by ship of many months. Undeterred, they all set out for England unaware of what the reaction would be to their gatecrashing of the event. They need not have

Australian Army
Cadets badge.

Canadian
Cadets exit a
helicopter after
an air experience
flight.

worried, as when word got out that they were coming, an invitation was extended not only to the Spithead Review and Bisley Meet, but to the main Coronation event at Windsor itself. With very little money between them, they set up a camp in a London park until the great day arrived. So impressed were King George V and Lord Kitchener with their determination to participate in the Coronation, both insisted upon inspecting them and even taking the salute from them.

Hong Kong Adventure Corps

The Hong Kong Adventure Corp was formed in 1995, and is a uniformed cadet organisation that aims to instil discipline, values and a sense of adventure into young people's lives.

Although it wears British pattern DPM uniform and practises many of the ACF disciplines, its mandate forbids it from undertaking military field type exercises involving combat tactics and weapons. Target shooting however, is encouraged. The HKAC is funded by the Hong Kong Government and the Hong Kong Jockey Club, with its main training facilities located in the picturesque Sai Kung national park.

Although a relatively new organisation, the HKAC in its short history has really made its mark. They also have in my opinion the best officer's mess in the world, located in a luxury suite high above the race track of the Jockey Club.

Unlike other cadet force organisations, the HKAC does not have the use of military vehicles for the transportation of its cadets, so instead relies upon an impressive fleet of private minibuses, commercial vehicles and high-end 4x4 SUVs. Their training facility features two Russian BTR 60 Armoured Personnel Carriers, which are on their parade square as markers.

Royal Canadian Army Cadets

The RCAC, like the ACF, can trace its history right back to 1861, and indeed followed much the same route to establishment, with the formation of units linked to schools. The motivation for forming these units was the American Civil War, and the threat of Fenian Raids around upper and lower Canada. These cadets units, or drill associations as they were known, were the humble beginnings of the Canadian cadet movement. Two of

A stamp commemorating the 125th anniversary of the RCAC.

Australian Cadets marching through Melbourne.

the first units to be formed were the Bishop's College Drill Association formed in Lennoxville, Quebec on December 6 1861 and the Trinity College Volunteer Rifle Company, which was formed in Port Hope, Ontario on June 1 1861.

Another fourteen units were formed in and around Ontario and Quebec, under the banner of Rifle Companies. In the early days of the drill associations, members were accepted from an age range spanning 13 to 60. Eventually it became apparent that there would have to be an age limit and this was set down in 1879, when authority was given to form 74 Associations for Drill in Educational Institutions. This meant that any young man aged 14 or over invited to join the institution would be exempt from active service. There were 34 Associations in Ontario, 24 in Quebec, 13 in the maritime provinces, two in Manitoba, one in British Columbia. In 1885, cadet support increased substantially following the Riel Rebellion, something of a turning point in the cadet force's history

In 1908, the Corps of School Cadet Instructors (militia) was formed to conduct drill and physical training in participating schools. All training was paid for by the Department of Militia and Defence. The cadre of commissioned officers was primarily made up of school teachers. The officer cadre was disbanded at one stage in 1921, and then reformed in 1924 as the Cadet Services of Canada, the forerunner of the current Cadet Instructor Cadre.

Cadets enjoying a ride in a Warrior AFV while on a visit to Germany.

Cadet NCOs on parade in the Caribbean.

1. Caribbean
Cadets celebrate
50 years of
independence.

2. Cadets get in
an M113 APC.

3. Cadets
visiting SHAPE's
HQ.

SUPREME HEADQUARTERS ALLIED POWERS EUROPE

4. Cadets from London examine a Gazelle Helicopter in Germany.

5. Cadets from Surrey ACF enjoy a ride in a rigid raider.

Cadets in Dress White presenting arms.

Canadian cadets from the Northern Territories.

It is estimated that as many as 40,000 former cadets fought during the First World War, proof of how big the organisation had grown. By the end of that war, some 64,000 boys were enrolled in the Army Cadet Corps across Canada. Following the Armistice, the Corps went into serious decline, in much the same way as the ACF. The outbreak of World War II saved the Canadian Cadet Corps.

During the Second World War some girls wore the uniform and solicited training as best they could – despite the fact that they were banned from being kitted out, trained, transported or fed. Canadians should not be surprised by this fact, as girls in the Corps can be traced right back to 1882 when they served in a Cadet Company known as the 'Daughters of the Regiment'. Girls were not officially recognised in the RCAC until 1975.

In recognition of the outstanding service provided to the war effort by former cadets – believed to number some 230,000 – King George VI conferred the title Royal to the Canadian cadet programme, creating the Royal Canadian Army Cadets. After the war a quota was imposed on the cadet forces, limiting cadet numbers to around 75,000 members. This forced the closure of a number of units. The outbreak of the Korean War brought an end to this quota system, and as a consequence cadet numbers grew again. More changes followed during the

Canadian Forces unification programme in 1968, which were positive for the cadet forces but largely lamented in the armed forces.

In 2004, the RCAC celebrated its 125th Anniversary in style – issuing 25,000 Anniversary pins to be worn on cadet uniforms. In addition to numerous high profile celebration parades, Canada Post issued a special stamp in honour of the RCAC. It is now a collector's item.

1. Derbyshire ACF's band in Malta.

2. Borneo band in Malta.

3. Dominica cadets form up for inspection.

Cadets in the Caribbean

One of the most fascinating groups of cadet organisations is based in the West Indies: the Barbados Cadet Corps, the Cayman Islands Cadet Corps, the Dominica Cadet Corps, the Jamaica Combined Cadet Force, the St Lucia Cadet Corps, the St Vincent & Grenadines Cadet Force and the Trinidad & Tobago Cadet Force.

All of these organisations have their own history, uniform and traditions. Some of these cadet units have been in existence for decades, whereas others have only been formed relatively recently. The one thing however that they all have in common is the fact they are all reading from the same page when it comes to working with young people. All have similar training packages to our own ACF, but with some local variations. However, when it comes to uniforms they are truly in a league of their own, as they bring a sense of Caribbean style, colour and panache.

HKAC ORBAT.

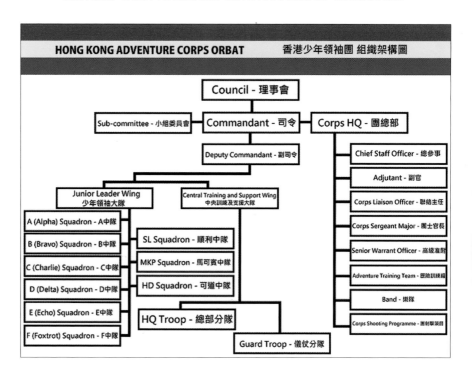

HONG KONG ADVENTURE CORPS ORBAT	香港少年領袖團 組織架構圖

Council - 理事會

Sub-committee - 小組委員會 — Commandant - 司令 — Corps HQ - 團總部

Deputy Commandant - 副司令

Chief Staff Officer - 總參事

Adjutant - 副官

Corps Liaison Officer - 聯絡主任

Corps Sergeant Major - 團士官長

Senior Warrant Officer - 高級准尉

Adventure Training Team - 歷險訓練組

Band - 樂隊

Corps Shooting Programme - 團射擊項目

Junior Leader Wing 少年領袖大隊

Central Training and Support Wing 中央訓練及支援大隊

A (Alpha) Squadron - A中隊
B (Bravo) Squadron - B中隊
C (Charlie) Squadron - C中隊
D (Delta) Squadron - D中隊
E (Echo) Squadron - E中隊
F (Foxtrot) Squadron - F中隊

SL Squadron - 順利中隊
MKP Squadron - 馬可賓中隊
HD Squadron - 可道中隊

HQ Troop - 總部分隊

Guard Troop - 儀仗分隊

RCAC logo.

RCAC cadet in Combats.

1. Setting up camp in the jungle is never easy, but this young cadet seems to have done a good job in Brunei.

2. St Vincent and the Grenadines Cadet Force on Independence Day.

3. The ACF visits Kenya as part of an expedition to climb Kilimanjaro.

4. Jamaican Cadets in ceremonial uniform celebrate Founder's Day.

5. The Barbados Cadet Corps on parade.

INSPECTION BY LORD ROBERTS.

Cleaning up day on board ship. Nixon

INSPECTION. BY KING GEORGE V

1. Australian cadets being inspected by Lord Roberts.

2. Australian cadets clean their kit during the long voyage to England in 1911.

3. Australian cadets being inspected by King George V.

4. Australian cadets being inspected by Lord Kitchener.

British, Canadian and HKAC cadets pose for a team photo on the Chinese border.

Australian cadets outside 10 Downing Street.

Bless 'em all. Tallest and smallest Australian cadets on the Coronation visit in 1911.

SIX FEET, THREE & FOUR FEET, SIX.

VIII

UNIFORMS AND WEAPONS

The uniform worn by both the ACF and CCF is functional rather than flattering. Long gone are the days when cadets wore elaborate ceremonial uniforms both in the field and on the parade ground. Today it is practicality that matters. The current generation of cadet uniforms is based on the British Army's Combat 95 design, which features a DPM shirt, trousers and a field jacket. The normal issue for cadets is two shirts, two trousers, one field jacket, one fleece and one beret. There can be local variations. Cadets are taught to use one shirt and pair of trousers for the field, and the other set for best wear. In the past cadets used to wear dark green trousers with an OG shirt as smart barracks dress but these are no longer issued. There are rumours that a replacement barracks dress is under development for both the regular army and the cadets. For formal parades such as Remembrance Sunday, senior cadets are allowed to wear No2 dress, which means a head dress, usually a peaked cap. In addition to these uniforms, some cadet counties also hold stocks of ceremonial uniforms which are only used for special occasions.

If we look at the uniform that was worn by cadets in the 19th century, although smart and flamboyant, they were very impractical. Cadets wore the uniform of their respective local Volunteer Corps, and these varied immensely from county to county. Uniforms worn by cadets within the Volunteer Corps were usually red, blue or green, the school-based units generally wore grey. Senior cadets were allowed to carry swords and even pistols on certain occasions as part of their accoutrements. The Boer War put paid to all these glamorous uniforms, as wearing bright red tunics made you a fine target for the Boers, who were crack shots. The colour of the season was dull khaki, a legacy of our time in India.

By the early 20th century, cadet uniform was basically the same as that worn by the British Tommy of the First World War. Known as Khaki service dress, it consisted of a khaki serge tunic with brass buttons, baggy serge breeches, a peaked cap, webbing or a leather belt, and hobnailed boots worn with puttees.

Cadets wearing a variety of uniforms prior to the introduction of DPM combats.

Although smart, Khaki Service Dress required a lot of work to keep it that way. The most troublesome items were the webbing belt and the puttees.

To keep the webbing belt looking green, a substance called blanco had to be applied, which was a kind of paste. Mention the word blanco to any cadet who ever had to use it (and most regular soldiers) and the air will probably turn blue. The belt to be blancoed had to be scrubbed clean first. This was followed by brushing the blanco paste into the webbing evenly, so a smooth, flawless finish was obtained. However, if you chipped it or it flaked off, you would have to start all over again. Puttees were long strips of woollen material that you wound around the bottom of your leg to prevent the ingress of water or mud. They were absolutely useless. If you wrapped them too tight, you cut off your blood circulation, whereas if you wrapped them too loose, they fell off. The only good use anyone ever found for them was as a bandage.

In 1938, the British Army introduced a new type of uniform, Battledress. Although made out of the same khaki serge as service dress, the uniform looked radically different. Out went the peaked cap, out went the baggy breeches and out went puttees. Battledress also dispensed with brass buttons, and the oversized webbing belt. Instead a thinner webbing belt was introduced which came from the 1937 pattern webbing rig soldiers used to carry their food, ammunition and water. The only item to remain was the bulky hobnailed boot. Battledress consisted of a short blouse, and generously cut trousers that featured map pockets. Head dress was either a forage cap or a beret. Linking the boots and trousers was a canvass gaiter, its purpose much the same as puttees. Gaiters were much easier to put on. Linking the trousers to the blouse were two buttons, which when you bent over

often sheared off exposing your back. Although better than service dress in many ways, soldiers often complained about their necks being chaffed as a result of the tight fitting collar. Woe betide you if you ever left it open without permission, as you would be on 'Jankers'.

After the Second World War came a new type of Battledress, slightly more user-friendly than the previous one. The key differences lay in better tailoring and an open step collar, which would allow a shirt and tie to be worn underneath. The 1949 Battledress as it became known still featured the 37 pattern belt, gaiters and hob-nailed boots, which cadets loved as they made lots of noise while marching. Battledress was also the uniform of national servicemen in the 1950s.

The name Battledress itself was somewhat inappropriate as it was impractical for field use on account of the material used. As a stop-gap measure until a more suitable field uniform was developed, an overall called a 'denim' was issued with the Battledress to protect it from being torn or soiled. Another aspect of this uniform that proved unpopular was the rough-textured shirt. By the early 1960s, Battledress had been replaced in the regular army by combat fatigues, however it was to remain in cadet service for a further decade on account of a shortage of funding.

With the ending of National Service, the army become concerned as to how it was going to recruit enough soldiers to fill its ranks. To address this concern it set up a review committee in 1969, which was given a remit by the Army Board to provide the cadet forces with better support, training and administration. One of its key recommendations was to dispense with Battledress once and for all, and issue cadets with modern kit and uniform so that they felt valued and appreciated. This of course was fantastic news for the cadets, and over the course of a few years, DPM Combats, cotton OG shirts, lightweight green trousers, green pullovers and dark green barrack room trousers entered service. Also gone at long last was the 37 pattern webbing belt, which was replaced either by a maintenance-free green nylon belt or a regimental stable belt. Cadets frequently have both items.

After reading this brief history of ACF uniforms throughout the years, you will probably be left with the feeling that whoever designed these uniforms must have been either a sadist or had absolutely no idea of what they were doing, as most seem totally impractical. But the durable and comfortable materials that we take for granted had not been invented. The current cadet issue of Combat 95 is a real blessing. Although still not fully issued to all cadet units within the ACF, those that do have it, love it. It is easy to clean, easy to press and if it gets wet it dries very quickly. I am a great fan of C 95, but still feel that a smarter barracks-type dress uniform should be introduced for formal occasions, as cadets like to have a special uniform for special events.

I hope the current generation of cadets remember what their predecessors had to go through before going out on parade. Just having to polish your boots and give your C 95s a quick run over with an iron doesn't feel like such a bad deal compared to what they had to go through.

Boys and girls join the ACF for many reasons, to make friends, to gain new experiences, to travel and, it should come as no surprise; to handle and fire

A well-groomed 1890s cadet poses for a school portrait. From the leather gloves and cross belt to the extravagant braidings, this is not a cheap uniform.

135

1. An early cadet volunteer's uniform, probably from the 1890s; more practical than the one on page 134.

2. Army cadet service dress.

3. Battle dress.

4. Second World War style battle dress.

5. Cadets in modern combat 95 trousers and OG shirts.

Cadets with foul weather gear.

Combat 95 uniform as worn today.

weapons. This is of course a sensitive subject. My own view is that far from distancing ourselves from the controversy, we should actually engage with it.

At one stage there were calls for our cadets not to have access to weapons, in the aftermath of the tragic Dunblane School massacre. The ACF was nevertheless allowed to continue with weapons training as normal. Some campaigners argued that if we taught young teenagers how to use a gun there was a higher likelihood that they may use one in a crime. I take completely the opposite view, in that as you teach young people responsibly about the use of weapons, you are at the same time letting them exhaust their fascination in a highly controlled environment. They are far less likely to want to handle an illegal weapon, let alone use one. No cadet has ever been involved in an illegal firearms incident.

All cadets in both the ACF and CCF are taught how to safely handle, clean, operate and fire a range of weapons currently in service. The weapon most commonly used by cadets both in the field and on shooting ranges is the L98A1 Cadet GP (General Purpose) 5.56mm rifle – which is an adaptation of the British Army's L85A1 SA80 assault rifle. Unlike the SA80, which is capable of semi and fully automatic modes, the Cadet GP rifle for safety reasons is only capable of single shot operation.

Before being allowed to fire this weapon, the cadet must first pass a Skill at Arms (SAA) test which is usually undertaken at one star level. To pass the test, cadets must demonstrate that they can handle the weapon safely and confidently. During the test they are required to make a weapon safe, show that they can perform stoppage drills unaided, and be capable of field stripping it for daily cleaning. Only then can they use and fire it.

So as to help keep cadets weapons handling and 'Rifle Drill' skills up to scratch, a non-firing deactivated version is also available at Detachment level. This is known as the Cadet L103A1 (Drill Purpose) rifle – commonly referred to as the DP GP. Passing your SAA test means that you can fire blanks while participating in field exercises, usually carried out during assaults and ambushes. In addition you can also fire live rounds on a range, which for every cadet is a great highlight.

For the older senior cadets who have passed their two star SAA, a more sophisticated weapon awaits them, the Light Support Weapon, or LSW as it is most commonly known. Unlike the GP, the LSW can fire in both single and automatic modes, which makes it being a far more demanding weapon to use. It has a longer barrel than the SA80, a bipod and a 4 x magnification SUSAT optical sight. SUSAT stands for Sight Unit Small Arms Trilux. By virtue of this sight the weapon is extremely accurate. The weapon itself was originally designed as an infantry fire support weapon to complement the GPMG (General Purpose Machine Gun). Its advantage is that it is both lightweight and accurate. However, it has one major limitation – its 30 round magazine. In modern warfare this is not enough, as you need to be able to put down a constant stream of fire. As a stop gap fix, a 100-round drum magazine was brought into service with some elements of the regular army but never with the cadets. Although the magazine substantially increased the fire rate of the weapon, it also caused heating problems with the barrel as the

Surrey ACF in ceremonial uniform on Remembrance Day.

Scottish cadets tend to wear local headdress rather than berets. The Black Watch (3 Scots) sport the red hackle.

The SA80 A2 Assault Rifle as used by the British Army and Royal Marines.

weapon was not designed to have such a high cyclic rate. As a result it has now been replaced in the light support role by the much more capable 5.56mm Minimi or M249 SAW (Squad Assault Weapon) as the Americans call it.

Before the Minimi was introduced into British Army service, every cadet LSW was recalled back to the army for service in Iraq and Afghanistan. Today the LSW is still in use in both countries, but in a new role, that of long-range precision support. Where this leaves the ACF long term is still the subject of much conjecture, as many doubt that the LSW will ever come back in the numbers that we were previously issued, if at all. This of course will create proficiency issues as both cadets and adults need to handle weapons fairly frequently to remain familiar with them.

As to the Minimi, I really cannot ever see this weapon being introduced into cadet service, as it is primarily a belt fed weapon, which the ACF historically has never used in cadet service. Prior to the LSW, the ACF and CCF used the Bren gun, arguably one of the finest weapons ever invented, and prior to that they used the heavy and cumbersome Lewis gun.

Over the next few years, the Cadet GP rifle is going to be phased out of both ACF and CCF service and will be replaced by a modified version of the new L85A2 SA80 assault rifle. This new semi-automatic weapon will be designated the L98A2.

The reasons for replacing the Cadet GP rifle are numerous, the main one being the fact that it has become increasingly expensive to operate and maintain in recent years as spares are becoming hard to come by. Also, smaller cadets often find the Cadet GP rifle difficult to use, not having enough strength to cock the weapon correctly while using it in the prone position (the only position cadets are allowed to use). The introduction of the Cadet GP rifle was nevertheless warmly welcomed by the ACF as it gave cadets access to a modern weapon that was unique to them.

1. An interesting variety of CCF uniforms; and perhaps a little too much self expression in beret positioning.

2. Cadets in First World War service dress complete with weapons.

3. Immaculately turned out officers and cadets of the late 19th century.

While serving in the TA (Territorial Army) I can remember seeing cadets training with this weapon, while I was still using an old SLR (Self Loading Rifle). I must say it made all of my troop a little jealous at the time, as we had been told that we were unlikely to have an equivalent to this weapon for at least another two years. So cadets actually had access to state-of-the-art weaponry before most of the TA.

Here are the specifications of the eagerly awaited Cadet General Purpose Rifle.

Calibre: 5.56mm
Action: Gas-operated rotating bolt, forward locking
Weight: 4.5kg with full magazine
Length: 773mm
Muzzle velocity: 930m/s
Effective range: 400m
Sighting: Iron sights

For the cadets, the key advantage of this new weapon over the old Cadet GP rifle is the fact that they no longer have to manually cock the weapon every time they fire a round, as it will automatically reload. By virtue of this, cadet marksmanship will improve substantially as they will no longer have to break off their aim to cock the weapon. This advance alone is sure to produce tighter groupings and higher scores on the ranges. Another advantage of the new weapon is its ability to use a custom Blank Firing Attachment (BFA). With the old weapon, cadets were

Battle dress CCF style.

not allowed to fire at each other within 50 metres, whereas with the new BFA-equipped rifle this distance is dramatically reduced to only five metres – thereby making training exercises more realistic and safer.

In all, the ACF will receive 7,500 GP rifles, an issue of one rifle per four cadets on county strength. Every detachment will also receive three deactivated Drill Purpose rifles. There will be three types of rounds available for the new weapon: Drill, Blank and Live. A .22 conversion kit will also be available, for firing .22 ammunition on 25m ranges. Because of the weapon's similarity to the LSW, drills will be initially based upon this weapon with some additions – making its introduction much easier, as most cadets are familiar with the LSW.

Shooting in the ACF usually starts at Detachment level with either an air rifle or a .22 calibre rifle such as a Mk8, which closely resembles an old Lee Enfield bolt-action rifle. Ranges used at Detachment level are 25metres in length and vary between gallery and tube types. During these shooting sessions, cadets are taught the principles of marksmanship – natural pointing, position and hold, sight alignment and shot release and follow through. The same principles also apply while firing the Cadet GP rifle, which is typically fired on 100m, 200m and 300m ranges. Such firing usually occurs on training weekends and annual camps. These range practices include the use of LSWs – if available.

For cadets who develop a flair for shooting, the ACF has much to offer. They can earn a range of proficiency badges and go on to represent their respective county at CADSAM, the Cadet Annual Skill At Arms Meeting shooting competition. The competition itself involves the country being split into two divisions. Although each division conducts the competition differently, it revolves around the same practices. First there is a zeroing shoot at 30m, a snap shoot at 100m and a gallery run which starts at 300m where the cadets have to fire two sighting shots and then 10 shots against the clock. After completing this phase they have to run to 200m and then fire 10 shots, followed by a further run to 100m where they fire another 10 shots – and all against the clock. It is a very demanding event.

Exceptional shots also have the opportunity to fire the L81 A2 Cadet Target Rifle in competition at Brigade (CTRM), National (Interservices Cadet Rifle Meeting) and International (Dominion of Canada Rifle Association Matches) level. Some competitions involve some international travel. For those who are truly gifted in this skill and have ambitions possibly to represent the UK nationally in the Olympics, a six-week intensive shooting course is on offer in Canada.

Of course not every cadet is up to this standard, so there are other alternatives for them to pursue, such as Clay Pigeon shooting, ETR (Electronic Target Range) where targets are controlled and scored electronically, and finally there

Cadet GP Rifle.

SA80 LSW, a rare sight in the ACF these days.

is the ultimate challenge of the DCCT (Dismounted Close Combat Trainer). The DCCT has cadets using a modified SA80 rifle fitted with a laser targeting system that engages various combat scenarios on a large screen. Effectively, it's just like an arcade game, only it's more fun and much more realistic as you have to keep changing magazines just as with a real weapon. It is a wonderful piece of kit that all cadets love using.

Cadets from Surrey ACF on a shooting weekend with the cadet target rifle.

IX

THE CCF TODAY

Like the Army Cadet Force, the Combined Cadet Force (CCF) is also sponsored by the Ministry of Defence – albeit in a slightly different way. Its aim is to 'provide a disciplined organisation in a school so that pupils may develop powers of leadership by means of training to promote the qualities of responsibility, self reliance, resourcefulness, endurance and perseverance.' It is not a pre-service organisation, although it is acknowledged that one of its objectives is 'to encourage those who have an interest in the services to become Officers of the Regular or Reserve Forces'.

A considerable number of Army Officers are from the CCF. As already mentioned, prior to the formation of the CCF in 1948 school-based units were known as the Officers Training Corps (OTC). The name change to CCF only occurred because the Labour government of the day felt that the name OTC was elitist. Needless to say, the schools were unhappy with the name change as they felt that they were the suppliers of officers to the Army, while their ACF cousins provided the rank and file. Today, the CCF is a lot more inclusive, with a growing number of contingents now being formed within state schools. Some CCF contingents within private schools have allowed local state school pupils to join them on parade nights, unthinkable in times gone by. In 2001, the then Minister of State for Defence responded to a question that was asked concerning the size of the CCF. This is his answer.

SECTION	NUMBER OF CADETS	NUMBER OF SCHOOLS
Army	25,724	238
RAF	9,439	185
Royal Navy	5,347	124
Royal Marines	in RN nos	18
TOTAL	40,510	259

These figures make for interesting reading as they show that the CCF is almost on a par with the ACF in terms of overall numbers. However, if we look at purely the enrolled Army figures, their strength is about half that of the ACF.

Most cadet ranks within the CCF are standard non-commissioned ranks, usually prefixed by 'Cadet'. The rank structure itself is dependent upon the size of a CCF contingent, and those with a sharp eye for detail will notice that there are a number of unique aspects to the CCF rank system. For instance, within the RAF section of a CCF contingent there is the rank of Cadet Junior Corporal (a non existent rank in both the ATC and RAF), which is equivalent to the Army section rank of Cadet Lance Corporal, this rank being created to give commonality amongst the various services. The CCF also has Cadet Under-Officers, distinguished by means of a white 12mm band worn either on each shoulder slide or on the rank slide of their Combat 95 jacket.

Officers in the CCF are often teachers from the school, and have no call up liability – unless of course they hold an additional position in the reserve forces elsewhere. All ranks are acting, so the highest substantive rank is that of Lieutenant. There are however exceptions, if the Officer held a higher rank while in regular service. Unlike the ACF, where officers running detachments are part-time volunteers, in the CCF they are deemed professional, as they are either employed teachers in the school or full-time paid instructors.

In addition to the officer running the contingent, a full time SSI (School Staff Instructor) will also be on the books as well, who is usually an ex-forces SNCO or Warrant Officer. The SSI is the only member of staff in a contingent not to hold a commission. Although the officer runs the contingent, command of it usually rests with the school headmaster. There are of course exceptions. Contingents can also

A cadet's not particularly flattering cartoon of his unit.

call upon the support of their local Cadet Training Team (CTT) – which is made up of regular serving NCOs. So staffing is rarely a problem.

A young CCF recruit awaiting a turnout inspection.

Cadets in the CCF enjoy pretty much the same activities as those offered in the ACF, but with some local variations. For instance, the CCF offers specialised military courses as a matter of routine, whereas in the ACF they are highly sought after. This is in part the fruits of the CCF's highly effective Old Boy network. In the CCF membership can be voluntary in some schools, mandatory in others. This of course leads to a great variance in standards – which is why you sometimes see boys in DPM uniform wondering around army camps with long hair and long faces. They are of course the exception, as the vast majority of CCF cadets that I have ever worked with have been both enthusiastic and talented. Eventually, the day will come when all CCF membership is voluntary – which will reduce numbers, but increase standards. As one CCF Colonel said to me recently, 'We really do need to go all volunteer, but I do not want that decision to be taken on my watch, as our numbers would plummet.' Many feel the same way. All, however, agree that voluntary membership is the best way forward in the long term. In my view, if the fear of falling rolls is that great, why not open membership to outsiders, especially if the unit is in an area where there is no ACF presence? I think it would benefit everyone.

Every school has its own story to tell. I cannot tell them all, as much as I would like to. Instead, I have focused on one CCF contingent and invited them to tell their story.

The tyre test, always a good method of challenging coordination.

Hurstpierpoint College

Drill was the only activity that Hurst's first Headmaster, Edward Lowe, made compulsory. When in 1860, amidst fears of a French invasion, volunteer forces were raised throughout the country, a number of masters from the College (including Baring Gould who famously wrote the words of 'Onward Christian Soldiers') joined the newly formed 13th Sussex Volunteers and the formation of a school corps quickly followed. Thus, on 18 June 1860 the No 1 Cadet Company, 2nd Volunteer Battalion of the Royal Sussex Regiment was formed and given the cap badge of the 35th Foot.

Hurst was one of the first six schools founding corps; few others followed. By 1870 there were ten and, just before the Boer War, only 42. Hurst's remained the only public school corps in Sussex until Eastbourne College formed theirs some 36 years later and it was not until the Boer War that Lancing and Brighton Colleges – aided by advice from Hurst – were prompted to follow suit.

Only a year after its formation, over 140 boys were in the corps and it was highly organised. In 1862, 60 boys joined the Volunteers on the Old Steine in Brighton and marched with them to a spot on the Downs near the racecourse where the

When a former pupil tells you they are going to pop in for a chat to let you know how they are doing, you usually expect them to arrive on foot or by car, not an Apache helicopter gunship! Old Boy Nick Barton DFC arrives at Hurst.

CCF 125th Anniversary badge.

field day involved a mock battle with regular troops. Then they marched back behind the band to Brighton Station and returned to Hurst after a 14-hour day.

As the 1860s continued, however, interest in the corps waned and numbers were allowed to dwindle until Britain's confrontation with the Russians in the North West frontier at Penjdeh in 1885 provoked renewed focus on the importance of military training. As a result, War Office permission was sought and granted for the corps to be reconstituted in September 1887.

Once re-formed, the corps grew fairly rapidly. The growth of empire, and the almost constant little wars this involved, aroused interest in military careers and the cadet force brought military matters into the very heart of school life. Between 1886 to 1896 some 80 Hurst Johnians (as former College pupils and staff were, and are, known) were serving in the armed forces and the College corps sounded the retreat at night in the front quad from 1897 until the practice was discontinued at the close of WW2.

Shooting began with borrowed K company rifles at Wellcombe Bottom, and the first class firing at targets was recorded on 6 October 1888. Corps training at that time was relevant to the kind of small colonial war which any members joining the army would then have experienced, and every effort was made to ensure that training was modern and realistic. A signalling section using semaphore flags began in 1894, and soon afterwards an ambulance section.

The government's decision to modernise every aspect of British forces, once the failures of the Boer War had been studied, had a deep impact and soldiering at Hurst (and in many other schools) became a more serious matter. In 1907 the Lee-Enfield rifle replaced the old carbines and with two ranges Hurst was able to improve its shooting. It was the conviction of the College's then Headmaster, Arthur Coombes, that 'every boy should learn to use a rifle.' In 1909 the corps became the Officers Training Corps (OTC) and was seen less as a broad training ground for military service than as a means to provide a ready pool for rapidly expanding the officer cadre.

In 1914, on the day term ended, the corps went off to camp at Mytchett Farm, Aldershot and they were there when the First World War came upon them. On 2 August they found all the officers, orderlies, cooks and even horses had gone and they had to fend for themselves. On Tuesday 4 August 1914, war was declared and the Hurst corps marched to Aldershot Station singing the year's most popular tune, 'It's a Long Way To Tipperary', a refrain soon to be heard in other dusty lanes and other circumstances.

Ironically, whilst the war inevitably made the corps a major school activity (numbers rising to 180 by 1918), it receives virtually no mention in print during this period although we know, from the school's roll of honour, the names of 112 old boys and masters who died during the conflict.

This dearth of information continues, perhaps more understandably, through the late 1920s and early 1930s. During this time, of course, the Royal Air Force achieved greater prominence. The first Hurst boys entered Cranwell and in 1936 the RAF Volunteer Reserve was formed with thirteen training schools and five flight schools and by the late 1930s it was the air force rather than the army that commanded more interest among those thinking of a service career.

The corps was a most important school activity throughout the Second World War. Boys expected to join up upon leaving school and the school's roll of honour identifies some 72 masters and old boys who lost their lives whilst in service during the war. In 1941 the OTC became the JTC and added an Air Training Corps for three years. Hurst cadet officers helped with the local ACF training and began to attend outside courses in physical education and as junior leaders. An assault course was created on South field and training became realistic with field days, night operations and patrols. Weapons training included bayonet drill and the use of Mills bombs, grenades, mortars and LMGs. There were courses in unarmed combat and knife-work. The Signals Unit, now properly equipped, became operational in 1944. The week before D-Day, cadets were involved in battle training at Newhaven with live ammunition and a correspondent describes how they could see the armada of ships in the port with barrage balloons hovering above.

Strong government support for school cadet forces continued after the WW2. The JTC was renamed the Combined Cadet Force (CCF) in 1948 and, at Hurst, an armoury and a small bore rifle range were provided. Kit and weapons were now the same as those in the adult armed services and the training bore a close relationship to what cadets would experience in their National Service or in the colonial wars still being fought in places such as Malaya, Cyprus or Kenya. As a part of the Corps Centenary celebrations of 1960, five members of Hurst's corps formed part of the 22 July march past at Buckingham Palace and the school provided the bearer and escorts for the colour party.

The Hurst corps continued to thrive during the 'swinging sixties' and beyond so that by 1981 the corps was 265 strong (out of a school population of 396 boys). To some extent this was due to Hurst's 'ex-pat' and military parents and to continuing entry to Sandhurst, now supplemented by army scholarships covering the cost of university education. But more than anything else the success of the corps through to the mid-nineties was achieved by its three commanders during this period: Michael Bailey to 1968 (who managed to appear at his farewell parade on a horse), Christopher Guise to 1986 and Michael Mance to 1995. Hurst's shooting VIII won many competitions including the Staniforth trophy in 1987-8, the Jendeveine Cup in 1989-90 and the Royal Sussex Cup in 1993-4.

Major Jim Gowans (now Lt Col) became Contingent Commander in September 1995. The redoubtable WO2 Fred Simkins, who had joined Michael Mance in 1994, remained as School Staff Instructor. Despite the odd wobble (numbers dipped to 45 for a while after the CCF became voluntary in 1995, the year when girls also first joined the school) Hurst's CCF is now stronger than it has ever been. The inspection of 2002 was an especially proud moment in the corps' history as the Inspecting Officer was both an old boy (1956-1961) and the Chief of the Defence Staff, Admiral Sir Michael Boyce (Now Baron Boyce of Pimlico in the City of Westminster).

At the time of writing, some 235 boys and girls are members of the school's CCF and over one-third of these are girls. A number of former pupils currently serve in Her Majesty's Forces, including Nick Barton who was awarded the Sword of Honour at Sandhurst in 2001 and, more recently, the DFC for his bravery in Afghanistan.

Late for Parade.

X

THE ACF TODAY

Today's Army Cadet Force is both well equipped and resourced thanks to its sponsor, the Ministry of Defence. Although structured and ranked in a similar way to the regular army, the Army Cadet Force is not in any shape or form part of the regular army or its ORBAT (Order of Battle). It is simply a professionally-run youth organisation that models itself on the army and its core values. The army does of course hope that some cadets will join its ranks, and indeed about 25 to 30% do actually enlist. The rest, however, just walk away with good memories of their time spent in the ranks. There is no call up liability. Not everyone is comfortable with the idea of young teenagers receiving military type training, especially some Europeans, who often refer to our cadets as boy soldiers, which they most certainly are not. To apply the term with any accuracy, look to the Lord's Resistance Army in Uganda, the New People's Army in the Philippines, Rwanda, Somalia, and a host of other areas of conflict across the globe.

Affiliations

The ACF is set up along county lines that have either a direct mass affiliation with a specific corps or regiment, or they have an open policy where detachments can form their own affiliations. Once affiliated, both cadets and adults wear the respective insignia, cap badge, beret/head dress and stable belt of that regiment or corps – unless local, individual or county area regulations state otherwise. For example, affiliated cadets can wear the cap badge of the Parachute Regiment on a black beret, but are forbidden to wear it on a maroon beret.

The most common affiliation is to the Rifles, with about 25% of all cadets now badged to this Regiment, the rarest is to the SAS, as no cadets are allowed to wear their badge or insignia. Affiliations are of course designed to be mutually beneficial;

the cadets solicit support from their sponsor regiment or corps, and in return there is the possibility of recruits. There are exceptions. In my own detachment, most of the cadets who actually enlist tend to join my former Corps, the Royal Engineers, simply because they have enjoyed working with them. It is a fact that if a regiment or corps provides regular support to a county or detachment, the cadets within it are far more likely to join them than anyone else. Therefore it is time well spent.

Ranks

Ranks in the ACF follow the same system as the Army, with one exception. The rank of warrant officer does not exist in the ACF because only a regular or TA soldier can hold a Warrant. ACF NCOs are deemed to be civilians, so therefore cannot hold this rank. Other than that, ranks are as follows: Cadet Regimental Sergeant Major, Cadet Company Sergeant Major, Cadet Staff/Colour Sergeant, Cadet Sergeant, Cadet Corporal, Cadet Lance Corporal, Cadet. There are some variations, especially if a detachment is affiliated to the Household Cavalry as they have a slightly different rank structure to the Army. Cadets are given rank as and when they prove themselves with respect to responsibility and leadership. There is no time stipulation or guarantee given for anyone to attain a certain rank. The ACF is very much a meritocracy

For those cadets and adults who are exceptional as NCOs, counties will promote them to Under Officer as a means of gaining valuable experience. It is an appointment and not a rank.

A cadet Sergeant motivating his unit during a field exercise.

A female instructor scopes out a target during a field sniping exercise.

ACF cadets usually wear their rank on a brassard if wearing OG shirts or in jumper order. However it is becoming increasingly popular for them to wear a rank slide on their combat 95 uniform. When using rank slides, the word ACF must appear on them, to avoid any possible confusion between regular army ranks and those of the ACF.

Another status symbol in the ACF is the stable belt. These are belts of the colours of the respective corps or regiment and are usually worn by trained cadets and NCOs only, not recruits. However, like many things in the ACF, there are local variations. In some counties, only senior 3 star cadets or above can wear them, whereas in my county anyone above recruit can buy and wear one as long their OC approves.

Today, the ACF uses the APC (Army Proficiency Certificate) pass system as a means of training and grading cadets. This has replaced the old Certificate A system, which first came into service in 1910, and is usually referred to as the Star pass system. Cadets work in Star groups. A cadet will usually start out as a recruit, unless they have previous cadet experience in another organisation. From there, they will work their way through the Star levels, starting at One and finishing at Four, if they pass all of the required tests, and attend all the expeditions and courses involved at each stage. Generally, cadets move through a Star level a year, but there are of course exceptions, slower or faster. It is a tried and trusted system.

Bridge building always identifies the team leaders, the team builders and the team players.

Cadet Force Adult Volunteers

Adults can instruct cadets through two very distinct channels – either as an Adult Instructor (AI) or as a Commissioned Officer.

Prospective Adult Instructors begin their ACF life either as a Civilian Assistant or as a non status applicant. They undertake a local Group/Company Commander's interview before being put forward for an IAB (Initial Assessment Board). Once accepted they undertake both a medical and an enhanced CRB (Criminal Records Bureau) disclosure. At this stage they then become a Potential Instructor (PI), and are usually invited to parade at a local detachment for further supervised training. Once the assessors are satisfied that they have potential, the PIs attend an Initial Training Course (ITC), usually run at County Level by a Cadet Training Team (CTT). Upon successful completion of this course they will usually be appointed to the rank of Sergeant Instructor (SI), unless further probation is required.

Further training will be undertaken at both county and detachment level as part of an ongoing programme to enhance skill levels. A further mandatory course that all SIs are required to attend is the Adult Instructors Course held at Frimley Park, which must be completed within three years of joining. After completion of this course, the AI is then qualified to be promoted to the rank of Staff Sergeant Instructor (SSI).

The final mandatory course for all adult instructors is The King George VI Leadership (KG6) course, which is a field-based course held at Frimley Park. On completion of this course, and subject to local recommendation, the AI is then qualified for promotion to the ranks of Sergeant Major Instructor (SMI) and

Buckinghamshire ACF commemorate their rebadging to the Rifles.

Cadet Adnan Edani aka 'Oddjob', formerly from Basra, Iraq.

Regimental Sergeant Major Instructor (RSMI). As with the regular army, promotion is usually based upon a combination of experience, merit, and leadership potential.

The other route into the ACF as an instructor is becoming a commissioned officer. In essence the instructor will follow virtually the same selection process as above, however once a Potential Instructor, the individual may apply or be nominated to

become a commissioned officer. To do so, as of 2006, the individual must then attend a Cadet Forces Commissioning Board (CFCB), which is very similar to an Army Officer Selection Board – although it is less physically demanding. During the CFCB, the applicant is assessed on literacy, problem solving, leadership ability as well as social and communication skills. Successful applicants will then be appointed a List B Commission in Her Majesty's Land Forces, making them a non-deployable Territorial Army Officer. During the selection/training process the applicant will hold the appointment of Under Officer, and upon commissioning they will hold the initial rank of Second Lieutenant. Commissioned Officers in the ACF will generally hold senior leadership roles that usually have more responsibility and commitment attached to them than those occupied by Adult Instructors. A commissioned officer will also have the responsibility of upholding the prestige of a commission in their personal discipline and authority – both on and off duty – as they are subject to Military Law at all times. For further promotion, Officers are required to attend additional courses such as the KGVI and the Area Commanders Course – all of which will help towards their potential promotion to Captain, Major, Lieutenant Colonel and Colonel.

Cadets and adult instructors often have military interests outside the cadet world, such as vehicle restoration. These particular vehicles regularly attend cadet camps and public events – one of these is jointly owned by two of my former commanding officers.

Cadet adult instructors Anthony Lindsay and Lee Sullivan survey the scene after a cadet attack.

Core Activities

The core activities of the ACF are: Drill and Turnout, Military Knowledge, Fieldcraft, Skill at Arms, Shooting, Map and Compass, First Aid, and Community Projects. As you can imagine, cadets have their own list of favourite subjects, and some of the foregoing will almost certainly not be on that list. But the cadet must learn all of them. Taking each subject in turn, this is why.

Drill and Turnout

The aim of drill is to produce a cadet who is alert and obedient, and capable of teamwork. It also provides the means of moving an individual or a body of cadets from A to B in a smart, military-like manner. The aim of turnout is to encourage a sense of pride in appearance and to ensure that once it is obtained, it never slips.

Military Knowledge

This is taught so as to give cadets a better knowledge of the Army and how it is trained and equipped to perform its role. Cadets are often taught about its illustrious history and its traditions, with particular attention to their respective corps or regiment.

Fieldcraft

Probably the most popular subject on offer in the ACF. Subjects taught include ambush drills, section attacks, Camouflage and concealment, field movement and signals and battle preparation, etc.

Skills at Arms

In the ACF, Skill at Arms (SAA) training is mandatory as nobody is allowed to fire a weapon unless they have passed their SAA test.

Shooting

Shooting is taught in the ACF as a means of developing self-discipline, concentration and confidence – and not as a method of encouraging aggression. .

Map and Compass

Yes, this subject is still taught, as it is always handy to be able to read a map and be proficient in the use of a compass, especially when your Sat Nav breaks and you cannot re-establish a link; but is also an excellent way of sharpening perception, mental processes, spatial awareness, and simple mathematics.

First Aid

For some cadets their least favourite subject, and yet it is the most valuable, as all members of society benefit from the shared knowledge. Cadets are taught First Aid to recognised standards and are awarded relevant certificates, some of which are earned through the St. John's Ambulance Service.

Cadets going all out to win a raft race, courtesy of the Royal Engineers.

Cadets making good use of cover during a coastal assault exercise.

Cadets practise house clearing as part of an OBUA exercise.

Cadets reacting to an ambush during a contact drill.

The ACF is not a static institution. Retired, serving and cadet Coldstreamers commemorate the opening of a new Guards-badged Detachment in Scotland by the Lothian and Borders Battalion ACF in 2008.

Community Projects

Being seen in the community in a positive light is key critical to success, as many people have the perception that all teenagers are not be trusted. To help dispel this myth and enhance public profile, the organisation participates in numerous community events such as school fetes, city parades and charity events. Involvement in such events is also good for improving confidence and social skills.

In addition to the core skills that are taught in the ACF, cadets have the opportunity to participate in numerous sports and adventure training activities: Football, Cross-Country, Swimming, Rugby, Athletics, Skiing, Snowboarding, Scuba Diving, Canoeing, Kayaking, Summer and Winter Mountaineering, Climbing, Orienteering, Caving, Mountain Biking, Archery, Paintball, Parachuting, Expeditions, Foreign Exchanges

Derbyshire ACF's Padre exiting a Chinook. He clearly enjoyed himself.

Gordon Ramsay enjoys a day out with some cadets; field rations, the use of, presumably on the itinerary at some stage.

1. Locally produced Cadet recruiting poster.

2. Many former Cadets are now fighting in Afghanistan, as part of Operation Herrick.

3. One Star Cadets celebrating the end of a long five-day exercise in Yorkshire.

Duke of Edinburgh Award

One of the most sought after qualifications in the ACF, is the Duke of Edinburgh Award. The Award programme consists of three levels, Bronze, Silver and Gold. The scheme is open to people aged 14-25, and involves a non-competitive programme of practical, cultural and adventure activities. Each award is broken down into four areas (five for Gold) which participants must complete successfully in order to receive their respective award. These are:

Service – Helping others in the local community.

Expeditions – Training for and planning of a journey

Skills – Demonstrating ability in almost any hobby, skill or interest

Physical Education – Sport and fitness

Residential project (Gold Award only) – A purposeful enterprise with young people not previously known to the participant.

4. Ranulph Fiennes flying the flag for the ACF.

5. Senior cadets launching an attack.

Cadets in the ACF are always encouraged to participate in this prestigious Award scheme as it is widely recognised outside the ACF world. Indeed, many employers view young people with great interest if they have been involved in the scheme, as it shows them that they have confidence, good leadership skills and the ability to take on a challenge. For further information, go to www.dofe.org.

Leadership Training

The ACF is naturally keen to develop its cadets into potential leaders, with numerous courses on offer to those who like a challenge. Current courses include:

JCIC

Junior Cadets Instructors Cadre is usually run at County level for those who aspire to be an NCO, or for those who have just qualified and want to make themselves more proficient. A pass usually means a recommendation for SCIC.

SCIC

Senior Cadets Instructors Cadre is usually run at annual camp by a CTT (Cadet Training Team). It is designed to assess all aspects of a cadet NCO, and is usually looked upon as a qualification course for further promotion.

Cadets open fire on enemy forces in the far distance.

Junior Leaders

This is run by the Air Training Corps (ATC) and is on offer to ACF cadets that are over the age of 17 and hold the rank of at least Cadet Sergeant. Upon completion, the cadet is awarded a green and Wedgwood blue flash for their DPM uniform as well as a Certificate in Team Leading, validated by the Institute of Leadership & Management.

Master Cadet

The Master Cadet Course is run at Frimley Park, and is designed to test a cadet in all aspects of leadership, teamwork and communications. A pass qualifies a cadet for a Certificate in Team Leading and the possibility of further promotion.

BTEC – First Diploma in Public Services

This is a well established programme that allows cadets to earn a recognised vocational qualification worth four GCSEs at A to C level.

Credits 4 Learning

This is a new programme introduced to the ACF in 2008 that aims to award educational points to teenagers for their participation in adventure training and outdoor pursuit activities. Basically, more points equals more qualifications.

Surrey ACF's Drum Major in ceremonial uniform.

Surrey Cadets carrying out a CASEVAC exercise in Brunei.

An Australian and British cadet enjoy each other's company during an exchange visit. Apart from the badges, the headwear gives a clue as to who's who.

Project YOU

Project YOU stands for Youth Organisations in Uniform, and is a Metropolitan Police Initiative designed to get young teenagers off the streets and into uniform – ACF, ATC, Sea Scouts, Girl Guides etc. It is indeed ambitious, as it aims to increase the number of London teenagers in uniform from 70,000 to 500,000 over the next few years. The initiative has the backing of Prime Minister Gordon Brown, and London's current Mayor Boris Johnson.

Outreach

As potentially good as Project YOU is, it is a London-based initiative only. Hence the continuing importance of the ACF's Outreach programme – which both targets and helps young people at risk nationally. I am the Outreach Officer for my Sector, so yes, I am a fan. In terms of value for money and sheer effectiveness, this programme has no competition.

Outreach features a number of projects that are adventure training type activities designed to encourage young, vulnerable teenagers to work together as part of a group. It involves the ACF, regular army, police and other social agencies that have an interest in helping vulnerable youths. Outreach is taking the ACF back to its Octavia Hill days.

> There is no organisation which I found influences the boys so powerfully for good as that of our cadets … and if such ideals can be brought before the young lad before he gets in with a gang of loafers it may make all the difference to his life.
> Octavia Hill, Southwark 1889

Cadets Today

Why do young people join the ACF today, and what do they enjoy the most?

Staff Sergeant Jesse Babri

I've been part of the Army cadet force for 5 years now. Being a fresh new recruit at the age of 14, it all looked a bit daunting at first glance, but I guess my drive to one day join the British Army is what kept me going. That and the family-like atmosphere within the unit (201 RAMC cadet detachment). I first heard about the army cadets through a friend of mine (Lee Sample) who used to go on and on about the kinds of things he got up to on a weekend away with the cadets. I remember him hassling me about joining, though he only did this because he would get brownie points if I joined through him; he left to join the British Army a few years ago. He joined the Irish Guards.

I remember my first impressions of what being a cadet meant: being able to shout loudly, doing a lot of press ups and having extremely high stamina.

Frimley, Cadet Training Centre (CTC), the Spiritual home of the ACF.

However, I soon realised that being a good cadet didn't just mean these things; it meant being able to work as a team member, solving problems using your initiative, having the knowledge of what a good citizen is and putting that into practice and being self-disciplined. Though these are only a few of the things the Army Cadet force make you strive to achieve. In my opinion, the most important of them is the ability to lead, inspire and motivate not only yourself but those around you and to trust in your own judgement (having confidence in yourself).

As a junior cadet I tried to be the best. I enjoyed learning new skills (most importantly how to possibly save a life through first aid) and being involved in a countless variety of activities; ranging from voluntary work to weeks away with the British Army. Though as I matured through the cadet force, becoming a senior cadet felt more of a responsibility than an achievement. I felt that, as a senior cadet, my priorities had changed dramatically, from striving to be the best above all others to feeling that it is my duty to pass

on my knowledge and inject this notion of 'be the best of the best' into the junior cadets. I found that what motivated me most was having other people recognise the progression and achievements of my junior cadets.

Sgt Pawan Katta

After three years in the Army Cadet Force, and at the beginning of my fourth, there is plenty that I have learned and achieved from being an active member of the organisation. I believe that I have made every effort, in the last few months, as a senior member of 201 RAMC, Harrow to give my time, effort and experience back to those who will follow in my footsteps and formulate the future of this exceptional 150-year-old organisation.

What I appreciate the most is the opportunity that being a small part of this establishment has given me to escape from the daily routine of 'school-homework-sleep'. Partially exaggerated, but the escape from that dreadful position to my current state of work-life balance has increased my self-confidence and social skills – which, certainly, are on my list of skills for life.

Furthermore, involvement in the six areas of the ACF syllabus – Map & Compass, Skill at Arms, First Aid, Drill & Turnout, Field craft and Physical Training (better known as the infamous PT amongst my peers) has added to my all-round development and given me several skills and qualifications. In the immediate future, these will enable me to differentiate my university application. In the longer term, however, I am certain that these skills will remain with me for life and enliven my years of retirement with fond memories of achieving marksmanship when firing the cadet GP rifle for the first time and lying under the stars, my heart beating away, on Annual Camp 2009, after narrowly escaping 'enemy fire' on a failed section attack!

At this stage I have achieved the rank of Sergeant. This places me as second in command within the cadet hierarchy. It is a responsibility that is tough yet very gratifying, which involves teaching and enforcing (in the case of PT!) the six areas mentioned above upon a group of 10 to 12 cadets at the

Cadets, dignitaries and a member of Parliament unveil a plaque commemorating one of the first Cadet Detachments in London.

A cadet from Surrey ACF bravely takes the plunge.

Cadet Sgt Major
Sean McCreesh
scoping out a
target.

After five days
living in the
field, a group
form up for a
Company photo.

two star level of the Army Proficiency Certificate syllabus. With this comes the responsibility to ensure the smooth running of a typical week-night at the unit in the absence of the Group Sergeant Major.

In terms of qualifications, I have been trained to use the L98 A1 Cadet General Purpose Rifle, achieving marksman status on this weapon; but also the Light Support Weapon, which has the ability to fire in semi- and fully automatic modes. On both of these, I have had the opportunity to fire live rounds on shooting ranges, but also blank rounds in combat scenarios. I am proud to be a member of the unit drill team, which won the Drill & Turnout competition at The Harrow School in 2008. I am trained in basic first aid with the St. John's Ambulance.

I can only hope for the eternal existence of the ACF, so that cadets of the future may feel as fulfilled and delighted as I do with my experiences as a member of this exceptional youth organisation. It is saddening to even begin to think about 'standing at ease' for the last time as my cadet career approaches its end; but it should be known that I will always remain indebted to the ACF for the life-changing experiences that it has brought me.

Sean Mccreesh, RSM

I joined the Army Cadet force in 2003 when I was just 11, was recruited by a close friend who highly recommended the organisation to my mother, who was at the time desperate to get me to be more outgoing, confident and to have more friends. At first I was reluctant to join, but eventually succumbed to the pressure from my mother, for which I now thank her greatly.

Through my recruit cadre I distinctly remember being the smallest cadet and being sick and tired of Foot Drill in the fairly big unit parading 40 cadets on a bad night. However now I am thankful for that as I pride myself in my foot drill. I was a very enthusiastic young cadet attending every weekend, every parade night and even coming down on extra nights to clean the unit for inspections. I couldn't get enough of cadets, it was like a good addiction; and I honestly still can't get enough of it.

My first annual camp was one of my best. It was at Thetford where I trained to complete my one star. On the last day I was presented with the best 1 star trophy on group parade. I was so proud to receive it and to show it off to my newly made friends. Through the next year I completed my 2 star and rather speedily did my second camp as a 3 star, which was very challenging both physically and mentally. The 3 star cadets are supposed to be the role models the younger cadets look up to. However, I *was* one of those 'younger cadets', being the youngest on the 3 star cadre at just 14. I remember people doubting the fact that I could manage taking on the 3 star cadre at camp at my age. But that made me even more determined to succeed and prove everyone wrong, and I did so. I felt like I was on top of the world, showing everybody that even the smallest of people can achieve the biggest of things.

Still smiling after five cold and wet days living in the field.

In that same year as a cadet I completed my JCIC (Junior Cadet Instructor Cadre). I remember having a conversation with an instructor from my unit who told me that my promotion depended on my course report. I passed with flying colours and was promoted to the rank of L/Cpl on the following parade night. A year later I attended my third annual camp to attend SCIC (Senior Cadet Instructor Cadre). I was promoted to the rank of Cpl.

Over the next year I achieved the rank of Sgt and attended the Cadet Leadership Course at Frimley Park where I can honestly say I had the best time of my life, making friends from all over the UK through the very physically demanding course, where you have to depend on yourself and others in various team building activities to complete the course at the Headquarters of Land Command.

On my fourth annual camp I was ADS which is Assistant Directing Staff, teaching younger cadets. I was promoted to the rank of Staff Sergeant just after receiving the best ADS trophy. This was another very defining point in my cadet career as I was proud that I had made such an impact not just on the cadets but also the Adult instructors. In the same year I was on the winning Sector Skills team for 20 Group. In the next year I was promoted to the rank of Sergeant Major and Attended the Master Cadet course, knowing that my future promotion to the Cadet RSM depended on getting a good pass. 'Showed immense courage through the face of adversity', is my favourite quote from my course report. Several nervous months passed before a decision was made on my promotion to become the Cadet Regimental Sergeant Major of Middlesex and North West London, a distinguished award for any cadet to receive as only one is appointed every year, to serve for a year before passing over to the next cadet RSM. I remember being rung at 5 at the morning by an instructor at my unit who told me the news; and he, like me was elated. At the time of writing I am still in my year as the cadet RSM in charge of 32 units across North West London. I have a lot of responsibility to be a role model for other cadets who hopefully aspire to one day be in my shoes, as I did when I first joined and Michael Haughey was the Cadet RSM, still in the organisation as an adult instructor. The most defining point in my Army Cadet career was being appointed the rank of Regimental Sergeant Major in front of over 1000 people on the camp.

My unit has had only one Detachment Commander in over 15 years and who has always supported me through the ups and downs of being a cadet, and who has always believed in me and encouraged me to do my best. That man is Sergeant Major Clahar and I am very thankful to him for his support over the years, not just to me but also to the unit where thousands of cadets have passed through and have only had good words to say about him.

As I am the youngest RSM there has been, I have the option to become a Cadet Under Officer (CUO). I believe there hasn't been one in 22 years. I still haven't come to a decision as to whether or not to skip this and just become an Adult Instructor.

If it wasn't for the Army Cadet Force, especially my unit in Acton, I would definitely not be the same person I am today. The Cadet Force had made me so much more confident, reliable, friendly, outgoing and given me qualifications, including BTECs in Public Services worth 5 GCSEs. This is why I wish to put something back into the organisation and become an Adult Volunteer, as a way of saying thanks for what the ACF has given me.

Cpl Isabella Ryan

Ever since I was a kid I always used to pester my dad to let me join cadets. Because he was the OC he let me come down to the unit a few times a month to see what they were getting up to, and on occasion I was allowed to join in with some of their training – but only the classroom stuff.

My dad was really into his rules and regulations and would not let me participate in the PT or fieldcraft until I had officially signed up. I always used to come back from cadets covered in mud as I watched them training during their field activities, but who cared, I had a great time. I always wanted to join cadets because I was always up for a challenge and I was always into sports, so the minute I turned 12 my dad signed me up. When I had first started cadets I wasn't that confident but I was determined to go as far as I possibly could.

As a recruit I never would have thought I would have achieved so much in such a short amount of time. After being in the cadets for two years I have been on many courses such as the PDA (personal development activity) with the Royal Engineers. I have been on two annual camps which

I have thoroughly enjoyed. After about eight months I was promoted to L/Cpl which was a great honour as I was one of the youngest cadets to get promoted. This made me feel more determined to go further. I have also been on a week-long work experience course with the Royal Engineers where I got to learn new skills and be with new people.

I have attended JCIC were I got C+ which brought my confidence up a lot. When I was a L/Cpl we entered a drill competition and our team came out tops. A couple of months after that I got promoted to Cpl which was one of the best moments in my cadet career because I had got my second stripe by the time I was 14 years old. I am also very proud of the fact that I have almost qualified as a 3 Star cadet already.

I have been abroad twice to Bavaria with the ACF on skiing courses, and am almost as good as my dad. I went to France for the 65th D-Day Anniversary. I have attended many remembrance parades and also helped out at the London taxi drivers' 'Mad Hatters' tea party for disadvantaged kids. I have also taken part in many sporting events such as cross country, football and athletics were I have collected many medals. I have also been to Trooping the Colour and to Beating the Retreat in central London.

Although I feel that I have done quite a lot in my short time with the army cadet force, I still feel that I have got much more to do in my four years remaining – SCIC, BTEC, Master Cadet and D of E. I will treasure my ACF moments for life, as I have learnt so much that will help me in my future career plans. I have also made many lifelong friends and have numerous treasured memories that will stay with me forever.

XI

THE DETACHMENT

The heart of the Army Cadet is the Detachment, be it in a hut, school, TAVR Centre, portakabin or purpose-built cadet centre. The type of building itself makes little difference to the quality of the cadet, as the most important factor in their development is the human factor. Any Detachment's success stems from the enthusiasm, dedication and skill of its commander and his or her staff.

Every Detachment has a unique character. Each develops over time certain customs and traits that each cadet and adult will pass on to their successors so that the unit identity is kept alive. These may manifest themselves in many ways, such as how the unit forms up for a parade, even what songs it sings while travelling.

Giving up two nights of your life each and every week of the year bar block leave periods is a massive commitment for both cadets and adults alike, so the sheer fact that everyone keeps turning up night after night come sun, rain, fog, or snow, means that somebody must be doing something right. A Detachment should be like a family, with all welcome. It should have no prejudice, no favourites and no tolerance of bullying, drink or drugs. Anyone who enters its doors should feel at home regardless of their colour, creed or gender. If that is not the case, then the unit has no place in the ACF.

The Detachment Commander

Arguably the most interesting and demanding role in the ACF is that of Detachment Commander. I'm certainly not arguing against. As a Detachment Commander with 73 cadets and four members of staff to look after, I am in a position to give you a 'horse's mouth' account of what life is like on the front line of the ACF.

As a Detachment Commander you are responsible for everything that happens in your respective unit – be it good or bad. It is your job to plan, facilitate, execute

Cadet Bunker presents a D-Day veteran with one of his unit's polo shirts as a memento of the 65th anniversary in Normandy.

and manage all aspects of the unit's daily running and routine. It is also your job to organise an interesting and varied training programme that will help your cadets achieve their maximum potential. You do of course have plenty of support from both your senior cadets and adults, but ultimately you are in the driving seat.

Cadets like to see their officers and instructors participate in activities as it creates a good bond between leaders and followers, so that's part of the work. It also gives them a chance to have a laugh at our expense when we get things wrong. There are of course times when instructors have to put their serious hats on – especially so during safety briefings and shooting events – but these should be rare occasions.

Cadets are a lot more clued up than adults sometimes give them credit for, with most clearly understanding where the line is drawn. In my own unit, I always give a briefing to new recruits as to what the standards within my unit and the ACF are. I make it clear from the outset that we will not tolerate bullying, racism, sexism, theft, drug and drink abuse or disrespect toward any member of staff. It is extremely rare for me to have to discipline a cadet for any of the above. It all comes down to the culture within the unit. Too lax and you will have discipline issues; too strict and cadets will be stifled in their ability to express themselves, and you run the risk of losing them. The best way to integrate cadets quickly and effectively is to make them feel valued and of importance to the Detachment more or less from the off. I often remind my cadets that our unit is not mine but ours, with all having a role too play. I am particularly fortunate in that I have an excellent support team consisting of both senior cadets and adults to assist me, to do it alone would be nigh on impossible.

A D-Day veteran from Harrow enjoys the company of cadets from his local detachment while in Normandy. This was the Army Cadet Force's largest ever overseas deployment. It was clear that the cadets and veterans enjoyed each other's company, and will no doubt treasure the memories of their time together for ever.

As a Detachment Commander, you are required to perform many roles. Typically; I am an administrator, an accountant, a fund raiser, a range officer, a minibus driver, an HGV driver, a part time social worker and finally a qualified instructor. I also at times feel like registering myself as a charity, but that's another story.

On the subject of money, unlike the CCF, which provides its units with an annual cash grant, the ACF receive no such direct financial support at Detachment level. Accommodation, insurance, water rates and electricity are however paid for centrally by the MoD. We therefore raise money through many avenues such as bag packing, livery companies, youth grants and subs.

One of the ACF's most generous financial benefactors in London is Jack Petchey. To say that he has been generous to us and indeed other youth organisations and schools within London would be a great understatement, as he has brought about a seismic shift in how we are financed. So on behalf of my Detachment, thank you very much Jack. Thanks to Jack's support, I was able to take a large number of my cadets skiing for the first time in Bavaria. Many of them had never been abroad before.

My Colonel once said to us all, if you don't want a busy life then don't join the ACF. How right he was. In 2006, he presented me with an award from a City Livery Company for services to my sector. To be awarded this was a great honour and I honestly never thought that I could repeat the level of commitment that I had put in that year to win it. And yet, as I look at my schedule for 2009 I am already well on my way to exceeding it. Over and above my two nights a week, and my one weekend away a month, I have already been away for that eight-day skiing trip to Bavaria, attended an eight-day Outreach event in Wales, participated in the five-day trip to Normandy commemorating the 65th Anniversary of the D-Day landings, and as I am writing this book I am packing for a 54-day trip to Canada as an exchange officer, followed by a seven-day visit to Morocco to recce for a future adventure training trip. It will without doubt be my busiest year yet. It should be stressed that the ACF does not expect or require you as an adult instructor to put in this level of commitment. It is simply a personal choice.

Recruitment

There is no such thing as a stereotypical cadet or unit. Units tend to have success cycles, just like a football or rugby team. One year they could be the best in their group, whereas the next time around it's someone else's turn. Although no two years are ever the same, there are curious loops that repeat themselves from time to time. It is however a very rare unit that can be consistent all of the time in every cadet discipline and event.

Units throughout the UK also have tremendous ethnic diversity. In my own unit, I have cadets whose family roots can be traced back to the Caribbean, China, Congo, France, India, Iraq, Ireland, Kenya, Mauritius, Pakistan, Portugal, Somalia and South Africa. We reflect our borough's diversity.

In terms of cadet recruitment, the best recruiters are the cadets themselves, as they say it like it is. In addition we also gain recruits from the ACF web site and from local community events. There is no particular type of teenager that we are targeting, as all are welcome. Once a recruit joins up and finds that they like the ACF, they will usually bring along some of their friends.

In 2008 one of my senior male cadets went on a one-man recruiting crusade around the local schools. Within days of each school visit, they were quite literally falling through our doors – and for the next seven weeks, I did nothing but host prospective cadets and their parents, a worthwhile effort for all concerned as twelve of them enrolled.

In 'Credit Crunch' Britain, despite the daily doses of doom and gloom, the Army Cadet Force is doing extremely well – with some 45,000 cadets, 8,500 Adult Volunteers dispersed nationally through 1,760 Detachments. Historically, the ACF has always suffered during times of economic difficulties. So what has changed? The answer is its relevance to society. In addition to its financial woes, Britain also has a problem with its youth. The reasons for this are many and varied and they are certainly the subject of much heated debate. However, one thing is agreed by all, and that is the fact that young people need positive role models in their lives and a place where they can focus their pent-up energies and frustrations. They do not have to look very far to find such an organisation. It would seem that finally society is waking up to what the ACF has to offer, and more importantly – they want to endorse it.

Education by Sheridan Bratt

Educating young people in a structured and disciplined environment has always been at the heart of the Army Cadet Force and Combined Cadet Force. It was recognised back in the 1890s by Octavia Hill that cadet training would provide young people (boys at that time) with the life skills and virtues of cleanliness, teamwork and self-reliance vital to helping lift these boys out of poverty and give them a better start in life. Over 100 years later, this mantle has been taken up by CVQO – the Cadet Vocational Qualification Organisation, which was set up to help cadets in all four cadet forces to gain qualifications as a result of their cadet activities and thereby give those who had little chance of academic success a vital start on the further education or work ladder.

The cadet training syllabus known as the Army Proficiency Certificate (APC) forms the rudiments of training in the ACF and it was this that was used to establish the basis of the CVQO qualifications. A survey conducted in 1996 by the Army Cadet Force Association found that over 45 per cent of their 16-year-old members were leaving school without achieving 5 GCSEs A*–C. A lot of these were 'disaffected' pupils. At that time, Edward Woods, a retired Lieutenant Colonel who had been Chief Instructor at the Cadet Training Centre in Frimley, sought to achieve a qualification for cadets based on their APC syllabus.

In the late 1990s with the support of Edexcel, the awarding body for BTEC qualifications, Edward started looking at ways of mapping the cadet syllabus to the BTEC First Diploma in Public Services. He found that over 70 per cent of the Diploma could be achieved through the cadet syllabus and set about creating the 'paper-based' additional education to meet the rigours of Edexcel. By 2001 he had gained support to run a trial for 100 cadets, paid for by the Army Cadet Force Association and CVQO was born.

The BTEC First Diploma in Public Services is a Level 2 qualification giving cadets the equivalent of 4 GCSEs A*–C through pursuing their hobby. It was only the first of a series of qualifications to be developed for cadets. Music, a highly important activity within all four cadet forces, was the next area for expansion. The small team at CVQO was joined by a music specialist to develop a similar qualification, the BTEC First Diploma in Music. This is now highly successful and operates across all four cadet forces. Engineering was the third diploma to be made available to cadets. This qualification is currently only open to sea cadets, but the real positive benefit for cadets is that they do not need to do any additional work other than complete the Sea Cadet Marine Engineering syllabus. This culmination of sea cadet engineering expertise enables cadets to gain a BTEC First Diploma in Engineering (Maintenance) rather than a proprietary sea cadet qualification. It is hoped to extend this qualification to more cadets in the future. As with Public Services, BTEC First Diplomas in Engineering and Music give young people the equivalent of 4 GCSEs A*–C and some cadets have gone so far as to take all three qualifications, boosting their CVs significantly. For many employers and universities the fact that young people have earned qualifications is important, but the realisation that these qualifications have been earned voluntarily, as a result of a hobby, in the cadet's own time is most impressive.

In addition to the BTEC qualifications which form the backbone of CVQO's cadet qualifications portfolio, CVQO has developed a relationship with the Institute of Leadership and Management (ILM) who recognise the valuable skills that are taught on the many leadership and teamwork courses for cadets. As a result senior cadets are now able to gain a level 2 qualification in leadership and management. This qualification is recognised by industry as an entry level management qualification and certainly not something that they would expect to have been achieved by many 17- and 18-year-olds.

Further developments within CVQO were realised when the adult volunteers revealed that they would also appreciate gaining qualifications as a result of their hobby. Over the years CVQO has built a portfolio of qualifications and recognition awards from City and Guilds, ILM and Edexcel. Cadet staff can now achieve a range of qualifications from Level 2 to Level 7 – the equivalent of GCSE – to a Master's degree. Expansion is constantly on the horizon, including a trial currently underway for an A-Level equivalent qualification for Public Services and at the lower end a Level 1 qualification to set cadets firmly on the path to study.

One can only speculate as to the growth and direction of CVQO in the future, but expansion from a three-man team to a staff of over 40 people offering a broad range of qualifications for both cadets and adults is certainly something that we believe Octavia Hill would have been proud of in her quest for social reform through the cadet forces.

XII

AN APPEAL

If you are a cadet or a member of the Army Cadet Force, you of course already know what this organisation is all about. If you are a former member of the Army Cadet Force, then I hope that I have brought back some good memories for you, and made you slightly jealous of what we get up to nowadays. If you are neither of the above, I hope that I have made you curious enough to find out more about us. If you are a teenager, 12 or over, take a look. If you are an adult, why not join the ACF as an instructor? We are always looking for good people. Remember: everyone dies, but not everyone lives.

In 2010, The Army Cadet Force celebrates its 150th Anniversary with Her Majesty The Queen kindly agreeing to be patron of this spectacular event.

In honour of this occasion, there will be numerous parades and overseas visits planned, so look out for further details.

As part of my contribution towards this event, I aim to set up an Army Cadet Force museum complete with uniforms, photos, memorabilia, weapons and interactive exhibits. If you would like to get involved in this project, please contact me, Mike Ryan, C/O The History Press, The Mill, Brimscombe Port, Stroud, Gloucestershire, GL5 2QG.

APPENDIX:

THE CEREMONY OF ENROLMENT

The ceremony varies from Detachment to Detachment but this is the official version of what should happen, as prescribed in the Army Cadet Force handbook. It is desirable that the important step of making the Cadet Promise shall be made as memorable as possible to the recruit. Any such ceremony must be kept short and simple and be dignified and sincere. The following ceremony is set forth as a guide to unit commanders.

Preparation

1. The ceremony will always be administered by the boys own immediate commissioned officer, ie the Platoon or Company Commander.

2. The minimum number present in addition to the recruit must be the officer concerned and two senior cadets who will act as sponsors. These sponsors should be older cadets who have been responsible for the preparation of the recruit by training him in his recruit's test and should be willing to act as guides and advisers throughout the recruit's subsequent cadet career.

3. Normally only one recruit should be invested at a time, and seldom more than four, or the ceremony may lose much of its force. When two or more recruits are invested at the same time it is desirable, but not essential, that each recruit should have his own pair of sponsors.

4. Before making his promise, the recruit should have completed his recruit's test, and the officer concerned shall satisfy himself that the new member thoroughly understands the purpose and meaning of the Promise. An explanation of the Promise should be given to the boy by his sponsors or his officer some days before the actual ceremony so that the cadet has sufficient time for reflection.

5. The ceremony will normally take place at the cadet's own headquarters on a normal parade night. It will never be held in conjunction with any display or public event or allowed to become a display item or used for propaganda purposes. It is a personal matter for the new cadet.

6. It is desirable that the setting be prepared in small details so as to help provide a suitable atmosphere. The centrepiece, for example, should be a small table covered with the Union Jack and bearing any regimental trophy the unit may have gained or other traditional decoration.

7. When the ceremony is held on a normal parade night it will be best held at the end, in order that cadets may disperse without an anti-climax.

8. When the remainder of the company are present the cadets may be paraded prior to the ceremony, the recommended formation being that of hollow square facing the table. Prior to the recruit's entrance the officer may like to remind all present of the nature of the ceremony and invite those attending to think upon the time when they themselves assumed the responsibility of the Promise.

The Ceremony

The officer will take his place, standing at the flag-covered table. The recruit will be brought to the officer by his sponsors and will take a position immediately in front of the centre of the table with the sponsors on each side of him but one pace to the rear.

Senior Sponsor: This is John Smith, Sir, who wishes to become a full member of our Company.

Officer: Smith, you have now been with the cadets for four weeks. Have you carefully considered what it means to be a cadet?

Recruit: I have, Sir.

Officer: Do you realise that as a full member of the Army Cadet Force we shall expect from you a very high standard – that we shall expect you to work hard and to play hard?

Recruit: I do, Sir.

Officer: Do you understand that by joining this Company you are not only joining a force which extends throughout this whole country, but that you are being made a member of the X Regiment (or Corps) and you will be expected to train and fit yourself to live up to its traditions?

Recruit: Yes, Sir.

Officer: And you realise that the tradition of the Regiment is founded deeply on loyalty to God and to our Queen?

Recruit: I do, Sir.

Officer: Say this after me.

(The officer says the Promise phrase by phrase, the recruit repeating each phrase after him, in turn.)

'I, CADET ......, PROMISE TO HONOUR GOD, MY QUEEN AND MY COUNTRY AND TO DO MY BEST TO SERVE THEM LOYALLY AND HONOURABLY AT ALL TIMES THROUGH THE ...... (CADET UNIT) OF THE ...... (REGIMENT OR CORPS) TO WHICH I NOW BELONG.'

Officer: John Smith, you are now a cadet and a member of the X Regiment (or Corps). We now give you the badge of our Regiment (Senior Sponsor hands cap badge to recruit or affixes it to his cap as may be convenient) which will serve as a perpetual reminder of our traditions.

And we give you this card (Second Sponsor hands card) which signifies your enrolment and confers the right to wear Her Majesty's uniform, which you should wear with dignity and the respect to which it is entitled.

(He moves round the table and shakes the recruit by the hand.)

I welcome you to this Platoon, and your sponsors and I will always be ready to help you to keep the promise you have just made.
Officer: Parade – Dismiss.

Staff Sergeant Jesse Babri of 201 (Harrow) with his 'Best Instructors' shield following an inter-service drill competition.

INDEX